In the House of Silence

In the House of Silence

Autobiographical Essays by Arab Women Writers

edited by

Fadia Faqir

translated by
Shirley Eber
and
Fadia Faqir

First English Edition, 1998.

Series editor: Fadia Faqir.
Literary editor: Georgina Andrewes.

ISBN: 1 85964 023 0

British Library Cataloguing-in-Publication Data.
A catalogue record for this book is available from the British Library.

Cover design by Cooper-Wilson.
Cover illustration by Peter Hay.
Typeset by Samantha Abley.
Printed in Lebanon.

Typeset in 11/13 Adobe Garamond.

Published by Garnet Publishing Ltd.,
8 Southern Court, South Street,
Reading, RG1 4QS, UK.

Contents

ぐのやり

v

Acknowledgements

ೲ◉ಌ

I would like to express my gratitude to Liana Badr, Salwa Bakr, Hoda Barakat, Alia Mamdouh, Hamida Na'na, Aroussia Nalouti, Nawal el-Saadawi, Samira al-Mana', Zhor Ounissi, Fawzia Rashid, Hadia Said and Ahlem Mosteghanemi for giving Garnet Publishing permission to publish their testimonies. During the six years that I spent compiling this anthology, I made many new and interesting friends.

I am indebted to the Middle East Centre, St Antony's College, Oxford, where the work on this book began, and to the Centre for Middle Eastern and Islamic Studies, University of Durham, where the work has ended.

I am also grateful to Georgina Andrewes and Margaret Greenhalgh for copy-editing the manuscript.

Many thanks go also to my friends Samira Kawar and Nermeen Murad for their help and support. I am also indebted to Catarina Lamm for her contribution to this book.

Preface

 ⸲ᘎᘐᕉᕤ⸲

The inspiration for this book came from the first day, 10 April 1992, of the fourth encounter of the Multaqa al-Ibda' al-Nisa'i (Arab Women's Creativity Association) under the title "Women and the Novel". It was organised by the Municipal Council of Fes, UNESCO and Multaqa al-Ibda' al-Nisa'i. Many Arab women writers and a large number of critics and journalists attended. The novelists were asked to give a testimony about their lives and writing. That morning, while listening to the moving words of Hoda Barakat, I decided to collect some of them in a book.

Most of the autobiographical texts in this volume reflect the attendance of the Arab Women's Creativity Association's Conference and were written for public occasions, which casts a shadow on their precise nature. Taking their rhetorical value into consideration, they were called "testimonies". The voice constructed is a voice conscious of its place within history and language, a voice negotiating a "pact" with the listener or reader.

To collect together thirteen autobiographical texts written before 1992 and 1995 by Arab women novelists from the Arab countries of Lebanon, Syria, Iraq, Palestine, Jordan, Bahrain, Egypt, Tunisia and Algeria was a project fraught with difficulties. Apart from the obvious practical ones, there were also those related to defining the nature of the texts. The starting-point was simply to collect good writing by contemporary Arab women representing a wide spectrum of opinions; through this a number of shared concerns emerged. Although there are general trends or patterns, the texts show the variety of voices in the Arab world today.

Garnet Publishing obtained permission from the authors to translate and publish the following texts: Liana Badr's "The story of a novel or reflections of details in the mirror: between awareness and madness"; Hoda Barakat's "I write against my hand"; Alia Mamdouh's "Creatures of Arab fear"; Samira al-Mana''s "Writing and the notion of searching for female identity"; Zhor Ounissi's "Birth of a writer"; Fawzia Rashid's "Writing and the pursuit of female identity"; Hadia Said's "I knew her when she wrote".

Hamida Na'na's "Writing away the prison"; Nawal el-Saadawi's "Alone with pen and paper"; and Salwa Bakr's "Writing as a way out" were written especially for this volume.

Aroussia Nalouti's "The essence of language" was presented at the Women's Creativity Forum in Beirut in 1993. Ahlem Mosteghanemi's "Writing against time and history" was published first in *al-Katiba* magazine, issue 5, April 1994. Fadia Faqir's "Stories from the house of songs" was published in English in *New Statesman and Society* magazine in October 1991, and was translated into Arabic to be presented at the Multaqa al-Ibda' al-Nisa'i fourth encounter.

Each testimony is preceded by a biographical note. The length of the contributions varies, but in general the texts are short and make it hard to draw conclusions about the writers, their motives, the "truth" value of their texts and how oratorical they are. In transliterating names of authors we mainly followed the choice of the authors themselves. Both the introduction and conclusion are intended to help the reader appreciate the writers' contributions. As a novelist, I aim to provide the reader with an enlightened reading of the autobiographical texts, which should not exclude other readings and interpretations.

The texts anthologised vary, some are multi-layered and complex, others are simple. The translations of the text, therefore, was no simple matter. Shirley Eber and I looked for the translation which adhered not to the letter of the text but to its spirit. When necessary a few changes were made, repetitions were cut and some additions were inserted to clarify the texts. Then with the help of Sue Coll, Georgina Andrewes and Margaret Greenhalgh we tried to make the translations as idiomatic as possible without uprooting the original from its native culture. Our common aim was not to harm the spirit of the texts but to let the different styles of the original text shine through the final English translation.

The past six years spent collecting the material and putting it together have revealed the lack of research on Arab women writers and the urgent need for this field to be studied in depth. Rigorous studies of the writing of Arab women in general, and of their autobiographies and biographies in particular, need to be carried out. This book benefits, and suffers, from its pioneering nature, but I hope that it will provide indicators which other scholars in this field might follow in the future.

Introduction

❧᷒ᷓᷤᷥᷦ

Autobiography has been extensively researched and discussed within the discipline of literary studies. There are many books and definitions of autobiography, whether generic or stylistic, that leave us with more questions than answers. What is autobiography? Does it have generic boundaries? Is it a literary text with truth value or just a mere text like any other? Does it have historical value? Is it the story of thoughts, spiritual growth, personal development or just art for art's sake?

"What is autobiography to one observer is history or philosophy or psychology or lyrical poetry, or sociology or metaphysics to another."[1] A scanning of literature on autobiography shows that there are two extreme perceptions of autobiography: the first is that it is some kind of presentation of reality, albeit through one person's perception, and the other is that autobiography is a mere text or even signs or ciphers – its author, his/her intentions and the text itself cannot be traced back to a specific point or entity.

---

1 James Olney (ed.), *Autobiography: Essays Theoretical and Critical* (Princeton, N.J., Princeton University Press, 1980), p. 5.

1

For the past twenty years literary critics have shown great interest in the subject of autobiography, and it is outside the scope of this introduction to discuss all definitions of autobiography, so only the two extreme perceptions of autobiography shall be discussed, which must necessarily oversimplify the history of autobiography criticism. Between the classical autobiography and texts like *Roland Barthes by Roland Barthes*[2] lies a multitude of texts with different emphases, including those concerned with historical, social, cultural, political, psychological and even philosophical "reality" explored through self-representation.

Philippe Lejeune follows a generic approach when he defines autobiography as "a retrospective account in prose that a real person makes of his own existence stressing the individual life and especially the history of his personality."[3] He argues that there is a pact or contract between author and reader in which autobiographers explicitly commit themselves to understanding their own lives and not to historical exactitude.[4] The life history created in autobiography, whether true or fictitious, makes a "rediscovered" reality.

Lejeune's idea of a "real" person and rediscovered "reality" in autobiography – although simplified in this introduction – would be argued out of existence by French critics such as Michel Foucault, Roland Barthes, Jacques Lacan and others, who maintain that a text cannot be traced back to a specific author, and that both text and self become fictive or even a series of signs or ciphers.

For Barthes autobiography is essentially a referential art and the self or subject is its principal referent. As a post-structuralist he equated the art of self-representation with suicide in his book *Roland Barthes by Roland Barthes*. The person is a symbol, the narrative

---

2 Roland Barthes, *Roland Barthes by Roland Barthes*, trs. Richard Howard (New York, Noonday Press, 1977).
3 Philippe Lejeune, *Le Pacte autobiographique* quoted by James Olney, in *Autobiography: Essays Theoretical and Critical* (Princeton, N.J., Princeton University Press, 1980), p. 18.
4 John Paul Eakin, *Touching the World: References in Autobiography*, (Princeton, N.J., Princeton University Press, 1992), p. 24.

"freewheeling in language"[5] and the "I" in the narrative is imaginary. To create the self within the medium of language is paradoxically to erase it and place it further in the domain of fiction and transitory representation. The self and the life are fictitious and the text itself mere signs on the page.

Although the problematic of representation could argue autobiography, as a text with "truth" value, out of existence, self-proclaimed autobiographies preoccupied with a "rediscovered" reality are still being written. Most of the full-length modern autobiographies published in the Arab world today are still at the stage where autobiography has an assumed "historical" value and its text is released to establish a dialectic relationship with other texts, or merely to put the record straight. Abd al-Rahman Munif's *Sirat Madina* is a good example of a "historical" autobiography.

It seems that the predominant idea in the Arab world and among many Arabists is that "autobiography is history, and, as such, it should rely closely on 'facts'."[6] This prescriptive view of autobiographical narratives ignores many variables, including the "truth" value of autobiography; the intention of the author; the writer's relationship with the audience, and the problematic of language as a medium.

Among all the full-length autobiographies and autobiographical fragments published in the Arab world today, the following two stand out because their authors are overtly aware of the problematic of representation: Aroussia Nalouti's "The essence of language", and Hoda Barakat's "I write against my hand". The following extract shows how Nalouti finds language elusive and hard to control, "All efforts are made within the complex and obscure body of language; the architecture of the narrative is made from and within it; characters are sculpted from the network of its symbols . . . for it is all this and not this."[7]

---

5 Roland Barthes, *Roland Barthes by Roland Barthes*, trs. Richard Howard (New York, Noonday Press, 1977), p. 56.
6 Thomas Philipp, "The autobiography in modern Arab literature and culture", *Poetics Today*, vol. 14, no. 3 (Fall 1993), p. 577.
7 See this volume p. 109.

To be able to understand the above argument, it is important to trace the history of autobiography within the Arab–Islamic culture. The autobiography – *sira dhatiyya* – is not alien to the Arab world in its different forms, whether *tarjama* (self-account of private life or curriculum vitae), *mudhakkirat* (memoirs), or *yawmiyyat* (personal notes or diaries). It has been known in the Arab world since early Islam, albeit in fragments of autobiographical materials mainly concerned with the public rather than the personal and private; still, as Thomas Philipp notes, "There is indeed an abundance of autobiographical material in classical Arabic literature."[8]

In classical Arabic literature there are autobiographical fragments less formalised than in self-proclaimed autobiographies; among them are: *Kitab al-i'tibar* of Usama b. Munqidh (d.1188), and *al-Munqidh min al-dalal* by al-Ghazali (d.1111). These fragments reveal even the personal life of the author in an almost "modern" sense.[9]

Many Egyptians and Syrians, such as al-Tahtawi, Ali Mubarak and Ahmad Faris al-Shidyaq travelled to Europe in the nineteenth and early twentieth centuries and wrote about their encounter with the West. Autobiographical writings of that period can be classified into two different types: the *tarjama*, which is a self-account of private life, and the *mudhakkirat* (memoirs). *Al-Khitat al-Tawfiqiyya al-Jadida* by 'Ali Mubarak (d.1882) includes his curriculum vitae and is a good example of *tarjama*. Al-Jabarti's work on Egypt in the eighteenth and nineteenth centuries "abounds with necrologies following the pattern of *tarjama*".[10] *Mudhakkirat* (e.g. al-Rafi'i's *Mudhakkirati*) are quite common in both classical and modern Arabic literature.

The modern Arabic autobiography began in the late nineteenth century. E. De Moor argues that the first modern autobiography in the Western sense was Jurji Zaydan's *Sirat Hayati* (1908).[11] Philipp,

---

8 Philipp, op. cit., p. 574.
9 H. Kilpatrick, "Autobiography and classical Arabic literature", *Journal of Arabic Literature*, no. 22 (1991), pp. 1–20.
10 Philipp, op. cit., p. 575.
11 Julia Meisami and Paul G. Starkey (eds.), *Encyclopaedia of Arabic Literature* (Routledge, London and New York, 1998), pp. 112–13.

however, traces it back to the writing of Mikha'il Mishaqa's history of Lebanon, Syria and the Mishaqa family in 1873.

In the 1930s and 1940s many public figures wrote their memoirs. These included Ahmad Amin's *Hayati* and Salama Musa's *Tarbiyat Salama Musa*. This was followed in the 1950s and 1960s by accounts of cultural and social experiences in different countries, like Mikha'il Nu'ayma's *Sab'un* (1959–66). Other types of memoirs are al-Aqqad's *Ana* and Kazem Daghestani's *'Ashaha Kullah*. With the publication of Taha Husayn's trilogy, *al-Ayyam* (1926–55), the autobiography in its modern generic form was established in Arabic literature.

Some critics of Arabic literature argue that autobiographical writing has declined since the mid-twentieth century. "It seems, in terms of numbers and quality, that the mid-twentieth century constitutes a certain zenith of autobiographical writing in Arabic, that this genre of writing and self-expression seems to have stagnated since calls for some explanation."[12]

Even a quick scanning of writing in the Arab world, including North Africa, shows that the autobiography in both its classical and modern forms maintained a strong presence in Arabic literature. This interest in self-presentation and documentation of life histories continued to gain ground. In 1973 the autobiography of Sayyid Qutb, *Tifl min al-Qarya*, was published. In the same year 'Ali al-Du'aji's *Jawla bayna Hanat al-Mutawassit* was published in Tunisia. In Cairo in 1974 Tawfik al-Hakim's *Yawmiyyat Na'ib fi-l-Aryaf* appeared, while the following year Mustafa Amin's *Sahibat al-Jalala fi-l-Zinzana* was published.

A large number of autobiographies was published in the 1980s throughout the Arab world. The following are a few examples: Abdallah Toukhi's al-Nahr's *Ruba'iyyat an-Nahr* (1987), Louis Awad's autobiography *Awraq al-'Umr, Sanawat al-Takwin* (1989), and Sayyid 'Uways's *al-Tarikh al-Lathi Ahmiluhu 'ala Zhry* (1989). In Lebanon Anis Frayha's *Isma' ya Rida* was published in 1989. Mohamed

---

12 Philipp, op. cit., p. 601.

Choukri's *Al-Khubz al-Hafi* was published in 1980 in translation and *Dalil al-'Unfuwan* by 'Abd al-Qadir al-Shawi was published in 1989 in Morocco.

The experience of uprootedness and of living in the diaspora has inspired many Palestinians to write their autobiography. Among the autobiographies written by Palestinians are: Fadwa Tuqan's *Rihla Jabaliyya Rihla Sa'ba* (1984); Mahmoud Darwish's *Dhakira li-l-Nisyan* (1986); Hisham Sharabi's *Suwar al-Madi* (1993), and Faysal Hourani's *Al-Watan fi-l-Dhakira* (1994).

The autobiography as a defined generic form in the modern sense has established itself in Arabic literature in the 1990s. More than thirty full-length autobiographies were published in different Arab countries in the past seven years. But most of the autobiographies published recently, even those written by well-established writers, are still preoccupied with the "historicity" and "truth" value of events. The following are some of the full-length autobiographies that do not raise any questions concerning the transitory nature of representation and the elusiveness of language: Abd al-Rahman Munif's *Sirat Madina* (1994); Jabra Ibrahim Jabra's *Shari' al-Amirat* (1994); Ra'uf Mus'ad's *Baydat al-Na'ama* (1994), and Nagib Mahfouz's *Asda' al-Sira al-Dhatiyya* (1995). The "I" created in the narrative is considered to be that of the author, and the self is created in the medium of language, not to be erased but to be immortalised.

For Arab women writers, the writing of autobiography is not as straightforward as for male writers. This confidence and certitude about the self and its position in history and language is lacking. Aroussia Nalouti's "The essence of language", and Hoda Barakat's "I write against my hand" are struggling to represent their ideas, but are fully aware of the limitations of representation and language. Most contributors to this volume wrote their texts to negotiate a textual, sexual, linguistic space for themselves within a culture which is predominantly male-dominated. To shed light on this process of negotiation which makes Arab women's autobiography and autobiographical texts distinct, it is necessary to place their narratives within their historical context.

Arab women live in twenty-four countries which spread from the Persian Gulf to the Atlantic Ocean. In the nineteenth century and first half of the twentieth century most of their countries experienced colonialism and resistance to it which was then followed by independence. Resistance to foreign occupation released nationalist and socialist sentiments in some Arab countries, but after the defeat in the 1967 war with Israel, the pan-Arabist and socialist sentiments began regressing, to be replaced gradually by Islamic revivalism.

In the nineteenth century Arab women began to benefit from the spread of education. "Before the middle of the nineteenth century there were no known published writings by women.[13] Arab women's writing and contribution to public life remained invisible until the late nineteenth century when Hind Nawfal founded *al-Fatah*, the first women's journal, in 1892.[14] "The writing and publication by Arab women of their own memoirs and journals is mainly a twentieth-century phenomenon."[15]

No one knows how many women's autobiographies exist in the Arab world buried in attics and confined to oblivion.[16] "Nabawiyya Musa is one of the first two women, according to our current knowledge, to have published her life story, which she began in instalments in May, 1938."[17]

In the past fifty-nine years, many autobiographies by women have been published. Among them are: Huda Sha'rawi's *Harem Years*

13 Margot Badran and Miriam Cooke (eds.), *Opening the Gates: a Century of Arab Feminist Writing* (London, Virago Press, 1990), p. xxvii.
14 For a good overview of the historical and literary context of Arab women's writing see the introduction to *Opening the Gates*, op. cit.
15 Ibid., p. xxxv.
16 For a good overview of women's autobiography in the first half of the twentieth century see Margot Badran, "Expressing feminism and nationalism in autobiography: the memoirs of an Egyptian educator" in Sidonie Smith and Julia Watson (eds.), *De/Colonizing the Subject* (Minneapolis, University of Minnesota Press, 1992).
17 Ibid., p. 275.

(1940s); Zoubeida Bittari's *O Mes Sœurs Musulmanes, Pleurez!* (1964); Bint al-Shati''s *'Ala-l-Jiser* (1967); Salma al-Haffar al-Kazbari's *Anbar wa Ramad*; Safinaz Kazim's *Rumantikiyyat* (1970); Zaynab al-Ghazali's *Ayyam min Hayati* (1977); Widad al-Maqdisi Qirtasi's *Dhikrayat* (1916–77), and Raimonda Tawil's *My Home My Prison* (1978). After the publication of Fadwa Tuqan's *Rihla Jabaliyya Rihla Sa'ba* in 1984 a plethora of autobiographies was released: Najmia Hikmat's *Rihlati ma' az-Zaman* (1986); Wadad Sakakin's *Insaf al-Mar'a* (1989); Latifa al-Zayyat's *Awraq Shakhsyyia* (1992); Layla Abu Zayd's *Al-Ruju' ila-l-Tufula* (1993); Layla 'Usayran's *Shara't Mulawwana Min Hayati* (1994) and, most recently, Nawal el-Saadawi's autobiography *Awraqi Hayati* (1995).

In addition to full-length autobiographies by Arab women writers, many textual self-representations have appeared in the pages of the press and been presented at conferences. The texts anthologised are perfect examples of autobiographical fragments which were written for different public occasions and with different intentions. These testimonies show that the need of Arab women for autonomy is becoming more urgent and is being articulated in different ways, including through such autobiographical narratives.

Although Miriam Cooke argues that "The autobiography is a less common genre for women, particularly Arab women, because it emerges out of self-confidence and a sense of empowerment,"[18] some contributors to this book have written their texts precisely because they lack self-confidence and a sense of empowerment, whether political or social. The need to define their position in history and locate themselves *vis-à-vis* the male master narrative, and to explore and formulate a separate individual identity has urged Arab women writers to write their life stories.[19]

---

18 Miriam Cooke, *"Ayyam Min Hayati*: The prison memoirs of a Muslim sister", *Journal of Arabic Literature*, vol. XXVI, no. 1–2 (March–June 1995), p. 147.

19 Without revealing what the women writers I worked with or interviewed throughout my career chose to conceal, I would argue that many Arab women writers suffer, or suffered from lack of self-esteem and its serious consequences.

The need which women feel to create their life history is probably due to their suffering the "double jeopardy" of being women and political dissidents in the Arab world. Women face the challenges of the male autobiographer under totalitarian regimes, and also the challenges unique to having a role constructed outside themselves and a "master narrative" superimposed on them. But whether male or female, Arab writers are all conscious of the presence of the mighty Arab censor.

The major political upheavals following independence, with the resulting confusion and loss of control over events, inspired authors to write their life histories. It is as if the self that "should" lead a modest hidden life is struggling to find its identity and define itself in order to survive. Abd al-Rahman Munif's autobiography, *Sirat Madina*, shows how all these forces combine where discovery of the self is joined to its affirmation and defiance: "The 1940s in Amman were long, heavy and difficult. The decade began in the shadow of the Second World War and ended in the shadow of the first Arab–Israeli war . . . the children during that decade grew up prematurely."[20]

This preoccupation with self-representation may also be due to fear of death, "not individual physical death, but the death of collective memory and past".[21] The large number of autobiographies published in the 1990s is a desperate attempt to protect and preserve the self and its memory. Within theocratic, military, totalitarian and neopatriarchal societies[22] the writing of an autobiographical text becomes an act of defiance and assertion of individual identity. It shows that censorship, in its attempt to turn a nation into a herd, may silence the herd but never the individual.

---

20 Abd al-Rahman Munif, *Story of a City: a Childhood in Amman* (*Sirat Madina*), trs. Samira Kawar (London, Quartet Books, 1996), p. 308.
21 Yusuf Bazi, "Sifr al-khuruj: al-sira al-dhatiyya ka qadiyya akhiyra", *Al-Quds* newspaper, issue 1730, 14–15 January, 1995.
22 For an analysis of a neopatriarchal society, see Hisham Sharabi, *Neo-patriarchy: a Theory of Distorted Change in Arab Society* (Oxford, Oxford University Press, 1988).

In his introduction to *The Modern Arabic Short Story*[23] Mohammad Shaheen placed the question of censorship at the heart of criticism of Arabic literature, and accused some critics of looking at this important question in retrospect or engulfing it in generalisation. He argued that, within Arab countries, censorship is the origin of the short-story writer's dilemma and the "unfortunate circumstances surrounding the genre". He goes on to assert, "Perhaps Yusuf Idris was the only writer who took the risk of exposing the sham of censorship – the origin of the dilemma – with courage and frankness."[24] Idris blamed the critics and commentators for maintaining silence over the tyranny of the censor.

By extension, the above argument becomes even more pertinent when applied to the modern Arabic autobiography. Writers of autobiography when writing their life histories attempt to avoid confrontation with the censor. An extensive discussion of the question of political censorship is beyond the scope of this introduction, but suffice it to say that some of the most prominent writers have confronted the censor and either their texts were cut, or they purged them themselves. In *Asda' al-Sira al-Dhatiyya* in a part entitled *al-Mukhber* (the inspector) Nagib Mahfouz describes the inspector coming to his house and escorting him to the police station to discuss an important matter.[25] This is where Mahfouz ends the details of this episode, without giving any indications of the time, place or reasons for the incident. That part of the text was cleansed so much that it almost became infantile. Mahfouz, like many other Arab writers, skirted over important political issues in order to escape the omnipresent Arab censor and the security apparatus of the regime.

The above question of censorship becomes more urgent if the writer of the autobiography is a woman. The social constraints on

---

23 Mohammad Shaheen, *The Modern Arabic Short Story: Shahrazad Returns* (London, Macmillan Press, 1989).
24 Ibid., p. 2.
25 Nagib Mahfouz, *Asda' al-Sira al-Dhatiyya* (Cairo, Maktabat Masr, 1995), p. 75.

women writers are still in general more restrictive than those imposed on male writers. The woman writer of autobiography in most Arab countries has to avoid discussing religion, sex and politics overtly. Among the contributors to this volume Nawal el-Saadawi and Salwa Bakr were put in prison for their alleged political activities and writings. "This eventually happened in 1989 when I was held in prison for two weeks accused of inciting the workers of the iron and steel works in Helwan to go on strike."[26] El-Saadawi was imprisoned under Sadat's regime in 1981. This experience inspired her to write *Memoirs from the Women's Prison* (1984). Her imprisonment was for a variety of reasons including her discussion of the sexual exploitation of women and her political views.

Any documentation of political events which might be embarrassing for one of the Arab governments was kept out of Munif's *Sirat Madina*, Ra'uf Mus'ad's *Baydat al-Na'ama* and Mahfouz's *Asda' al-Sira al-Dhatiyya*. In *Baydat al-Na'ama*, however, Ra'uf Mus'ad's intention was to write the erotic history of a communist activist: "I think that whoever wants to write has to place a distance between his writing and his political and moral views."[27] The text is abundant with the erotic experiences of the author, but the political and historical content has been kept vague and to the minimum. Judging by the warm reception and wide distribution of *Baydat al-Na'ama*, the male censor in most parts of the Arab world has turned a blind eye to the sexual trespasses of the protagonist "I", especially because they are those of a male.

The role prescribed for the Arab boy is different from that prescribed for the Arab girl. "Because we are a society which represses its emotions and feelings, we consider the question of love between the sexes taboo and something which has to be avoided."[28] In her testimony Liana Badr writes, "When I was in the first years of

---

26 See this volume pp. 35–6.
27 Ra'uf Mus'ad, *Baydat al-Na'ama* (Green Life Centre, 1994), p. 99 (my translation).
28 Kayri Shalabi, "Li-hatha lam na'rif fan al-sira al-dhatiyya", *Al-Quds* newspaper, issue 1914, 4 July 1995 (my translation).

flowering, my mother warned me against standing for too long in front of the mirror. She elaborated her point by explaining that desire is a dangerous thing for a girl in our society."[29]

The application of social standards and restrictions is done selectively and depends on whether the "culprit" is male or female, poor or rich, middle- or lower- or working-class, in short, disadvantaged or not.[30] The male is generally encouraged to have double standards and satisfy, albeit in secret, his sexual needs. But the girl has no future without her "virginity" which is a prerequisite for marriage, without which she has no recognition or legitimacy within her community. So penalising female sexual activities is the main method of preserving social and religious order within most Arab societies.[31]

There is a kind of censorship that is applicable to women only: being accused of having no *sharaf* (honour). For some reason, women's honour carries more weight than men's honour. A good Muslim woman must be *mastura*, a word meaning "chaste", with connotations of "hidden" and "silent". Breaking that silence and speaking out has a heavy price. The history of the censorship of women's writing by the social, political and religious institutions has yet to be written. Some women who dare to cross the sexual, textual divide suffer slander, prohibition and imprisonment.

To cross the defined border and encroach into traditionally male space is to risk being accused of being a loose woman, a whore, a belly-dancer. Some women writers have even been held legally responsible for their fictitious creations. Layla Ba'lbaki, a Lebanese writer who was accused of offending the public taste in her novel *A*

---

29 See this volume p. 27.
30 Women could be both lower class and disadvantaged. For more discussion of the feminisation of poverty see the work of Camillia el-Solh. See also *al-Raida*'s special issue on Arab women and poverty, vol. XIV, no. 77, (Spring 1997).
31 Hisham Sharabi presents a good analysis of the male-dominated Arab society. See for example, *Muqadima li Dirasat al-Mujtam' al-'Arabi* (Beirut, al-Ahliyya li-l-Nashr wa-l-Tawzi', 1975).

Ship of Kindness to the Moon, said: "In Lebanon, a woman who writes is like a woman who belly dances in a cabaret."

While male writers' frequent use of explicit images goes largely unpunished, as the writing of Ra'uf Mus'ad in his autobiography, or Salim Matar in his novel *Imr'at al-Qarura* (1990) and Janan Jasim Hallawi in *Ya Kukati* (1991) shows, Arab women face much tougher measures in some Arab countries. In the United Arab Emirates, Zabya Khamis was put in jail for the writing of allegedly transgressive poetry. The Lebanese writer Hanan el-Sheikh's third novel, *The Story of Zahra*, was banned in most Arab countries. The writings of Nawal el-Saadawi were also banned in many Arab countries.

Suhair el-Tal, a Jordanian journalist and novelist, was accused of offending public taste by using a phallic image in one of her short stories. El-Tal was taken to court and, after a long, bitter struggle, was sentenced to short imprisonment, a JD500 fine, and the loss of all her civil rights. The following extract is from a published letter of el-Tal, dated May 1989,

> And thus they took me back to court to face the most torturing cross-examination in every session. There is an incredible insistence on convicting me as if I am responsible for all social and moral degeneration. The grave legislative precedence of accusation and possible conviction is a threat to a simple human right, namely freedom of expression. It will be enough for any man to claim that a writer is giving offence for her to be put on trial.[32]

There are many factors which contribute to this duality, including the specificity of the Arab–Islamic culture. Farzaneh Milani, writing specifically about Iranian culture but making points which can be applied across Arab–Islamic culture, stated that it has no "tradition

---

32 Asma Khader, "Muhakamat Katibat Qisa" (The trial of a woman short-story writer), *Nun* magazine, AWSA Quarterly, no. 1 (May 1989), pp. 26–31.

of confession, in either its catholic or secular sense",[33] and has sup-
pressed the public disclosure of self. The public and private spaces
are neatly divided in many Arab countries, especially now with Islamic
revivalism. To expose the inner self publicly, is to risk losing the respect
of the family, immediate community and society at large. When writers
commit their lives to paper they go against a culture which is based
on concealment.

Women living in most Arab societies today are suffering from
these pressures to hide themselves. "Muslim sexuality is territorial:
its regulatory mechanisms consist primarily of a strict allocation of
space to each sex."[34] Women autobiographers by definition challenge
this allocation of space and prescription of roles for women. Zhor
Ounissi presents a subtle argument against the imposition of religious
values on women: "We are for the progression of women, they said,
and their education, but on condition that this is within a framework
of religious and moral values . . . a framework . . . is always limited
by its angles and its dimensions."[35]

The challenges of being female in Arab–Islamic societies motivate
many women to write about their lives or how they perceive them to
be. They have been deliberately kept out of the public arena and
"have a still more restrained relation to public self-representation".[36]
But what comes through in their writing are the hard lessons they
have learnt precisely because of this exclusion.

Writers of autobiography within the Arab–Islamic culture of
today have, to a varying degree, managed to reach an epistemological
break with the past. Autobiography is written when the author steps

33 Farzaneh Milani, "Veiled voices: women's autobiographies in Iran" in
   Afsaneh Najmabadi, *Women's Autobiographies in Contemporary Iran*,
   (Cambridge, Mass., Harvard University Press, 1995), pp. 2–3.
34 Fatima Mernissi, *Beyond the Veil* (London, Al Saqi Books, 1985),
   p. 137.
35 See this volume p. 146.
36 Farzaneh Milani, "Veiled voices: women's autobiographies in Iran" in
   Afsaneh Najmabadi, ed., *Women's Autobiographies in Contemporary Iran*,
   (Cambridge, Mass., Harvard University Press, 1995), p. 4.

beyond the conditions of his/her group, overcoming the obstacles of an angry family, indignant relatives and a prohibitive society. The writer "announces his presence as an independent memory in an independent body".[37]

Women autobiographers have clear intentions of writing the histories of self and body, but there is a discrepancy between their intentions and the texts written. In this anthology all contributions are guilty of self-censorship, but some more than others. Hadia Said fell from grace through writing. "Her first book was like [committing] the original sin." She used the third person to describe the writer: "She freed herself from the challenge of Qur'anic verses, instructions and sacred epistles. She began to know. She began to assess. She became a writer." That sense of initial freedom did not last long and Hadia Said's awareness of the oppressive and discriminatory conditions around her led her to censor herself: "She had not specified the place as he [a male critic] had decreed, to ward off personal fears and embarrassment. And in drawing her characters, she had taken so-and-so's anger into consideration."[38]

Ra'uf Mus'ad enjoys and takes pride in describing his sexual encounters, without taking anyone's anger into consideration, "Sometimes she would stick her breasts in my arms . . . I would slip my arm under her wide dress and feel her warm flesh while we are studying the conquering of Egypt."[39] Arab women, especially those who grew up in the 1950s, are quick to apply the scissors to their texts to purify them of any hints of sexual encounters. In their autobiographies *Rihla Jabaliyya Rihla Sa'ba* and *Shara't Mulawwana* Fadwa Tuqan and Layla 'Usayran are busy concealing their lives. When it comes to the intimate personal issues history and geography are dropped and the text becomes lyrical, fictitious and illusory.

---

37 Yusif Bazi, "Sifr al-khuruj: al-sira al-dhatiyya ka qadiyya akhiyra", *Al-Quds* newspaper, issue 1730, 14–15 January 1995.
38 See this volume p. 138.
39 Ra'uf Mus'ad, *Baydat al-Na'ama* (Green Life Centre, 1994), p. 50 (my translation).

Although *Shara't Mulawwana* is more politically candid than *Baydat al-Na'ama*, it is a text dextrous in concealing the protagonist "I"'s sexual encounters. Describing her relationship with Amin, Layla 'Usayran writes, "I began to feel agitated with the way we meet. If he wants a temporary relationship, why does he insist on meeting daily?"[40] Later on in the text 'Usayran defends herself against the accusation of not being explicit and censoring herself, "They said she is not yet liberated; she has not revealed her sexual secrets. I replied that emancipation is liberating the mind and the deeds."[41]

As for the Palestinian poet Fadwa Tuqan, in the first volume of her autobiography *Rihla Jabaliyya Rihla Sa'ba*, she goes further than Layla 'Usayran, who mainly described her relationship with Amin, who later on became her husband. She describes an extramarital relationship with A. G. in Oxford. "But I was made happy and I made someone else happy. I realised my existence even if for a limited period . . . it was a splendid experience, whose memory will radiate warmth in my heart."[42]

But is the above a simplification of a more complex set of variables? Is it just a question of self-censorship or a fundamental difference between how women perceive themselves and how they articulate their experiences? So is there any difference between autobiographies written by men and those written by women? Has female speech been repressed by neopatriarchy and, if it has, how has that affected women's relationship to writing? Is there an Arabic language which is particular to women and different from that of men?

Different critics present different readings or definitions of women's autobiography. Georg Misch's definition of autobiography is considered "normative".[43] The success of any particular autobiography

---

40 Layla 'Usayran, *Shara't Mulawwana Min Hayati* (London, Riad el-Rayyes, 1994), p. 154 (my translation).

41 Ibid., p. 193 (my translation).

42 Tuqan, Fadwa, *Rihla Jabaliyya Rihla Sa'ba*, 2nd edn (Amman, Dar al-Shuruq li-l-Nashr wa-l-Tawzi'), 1985, p. 202 (my translation).

43 This paragraph is based on Sidonie Smith's reading of the different positions of critics on the question of women's autobiography.

is seen in the relationship of the writer of autobiography to the arena of public life and discourse: "Yet patriarchal notions of women's inherent nature and consequent social role have denied or severely proscribed her access to public space."[44] As a result her relationship to writing has been contaminated, and when she articulates the self and trespasses on public space, she challenges cultural conceptions of women's role. Because of this women writers of autobiography might assume a "male selfhood" and, therefore, their life histories might become representative of men's lives.

Women's specific relationship to the genre is seen by some, like Virginia Woolf, as only thematic, reflected in the content, which is determined by their subordinate position in society.[45] To deconstruct the patriarchal hegemony feminist literary critics turned their attention to "considering how the autobiographer's identity as woman within the symbolic order of patriarchy affects her relationship to generic possibilities – to the autobiographical impulse, to the structuring of content, to the reading and the writing of the self."[46]

According to Smith, "the autobiographer who is a woman must suspend herself between paternal and maternal narratives, those fictions of male and female selfhood that permeate her historical moment."[47] Then the "I" who is a woman is a product of history and psycho-sexual phenomena. The tension between the ideal woman and the ideal man manifests itself in women's autobiography. Women writers of autobiography move from the margins of culture towards the centre in order to engage in a "master narrative" that assumes the speaking subject as always male.[48]

---

44 Sidonie Smith, *A Poetics of Women's Autobiography: Marginality and the Fictions of Self-Representation* (Bloomington, Indiana University Press, 1987), p. 7.
45 Mary Eagleton, *Feminist Literary Theory: a Reader* (Oxford, Basil Blackwell, 1986), p. 225.
46 Sidonie Smith, *A Poetics of Women's Autobiography: Marginality and the Fictions of Self-Representation* (Bloomington, Indiana University Press, 1987), p. 17.
47 Ibid., p. 19.
48 Ibid., p. 9.

The length of the testimonies in this book varies, but in general they are short and make it hard to draw final conclusions about the writers, their motives, the "truth" value of their texts and how oratorical they are. The majority of texts in this book were written in Arabic for an Arab audience and then had been translated into English, to be placed within another culture and literary tradition, and at times it is extremely difficult to illustrate the above argument without the reader having access to the original Arabic.

Fawzia Rashid's and Zhor Ounissi's testimonies, however, are perfect examples of how this tension between the voice of the ideal woman and the ideal man plays itself out, and their texts are clearly influenced by the male "master narrative". The Arabic language is misogynist and whenever the gender is not clear the masculine overpowers the feminine. In "Birth of a writer", Ounissi refers to herself as male, "How hard it is for the writer to introduce *himself*. An even harder exercise for a creative person to present a statement about himself – near impossible that it should be in the form of a straightforward autobiography" [my italics].[49]

Again, it is hard to illustrate this point without going back to the original Arabic, but many of the attributes of the original text can be seen, and readers are encouraged to compare the different testimonies in this anthology in order to establish the linguistic and stylistic differences between them. Fawzia Rashid's text is an attempt to vindicate and validate the self, and is addressed to an invisible hostile male audience. In order to appease this male audience it is important to show that women writers (in this case Rashid) have not only mastered the language of male intellectuals, but have appropriated their ideas. Her main concern in "Writing and the pursuit of female identity" is "the desire to destroy a 'false' image"[50] as shown in the following quotation: "Question: does the creative Arab woman still revolve

---

49 See this volume p. 109.
50 Farzaneh Milani, "Veiled voices: women's autobiographies in Iran" in Afsaneh Najmabadi (ed.), *Women's Autobiographies in Contemporary Iran*, (Cambridge, Mass., Harvard University Press, 1995), p. 13.

in an orbit of limited and confined dimensions? And the answer: no, because women's writing today asserts the opposite of this and, in the coming years, will assert that she is more vigilant than previously thought in the search for creative, spiritual and intellectual maturity."[51]

Sheila Rowbotham argues in her book *Women's Consciousness; Man's World* that women's consciousness is fashioned according to cultural representation.[52] As a result women develop two selves; one is culturally defined and the other is different from cultural prescription. This alienation from the historical and cultural self is precisely what motivates women to write their autobiographies: "Women's autobiography comes alive as a literary tradition of self-creation when we approach its texts from a psycho-political perspective based in the lives of women."[53]

In her testimony Hadia Said explores this tension between the two selves: the woman who has a culturally defined role and the writer who exists outside the parameters of culture and who is writing within an Arab–Islamic tradition. Hoda Barakat is also aware of the historical and cultural alienation of women and the constructed cultural roles for them: "We write, I write, from a dual perspective, because I am a woman and want to resemble a man, to cut short the time for training and amateurism, and prove my intellectual ability to construct and to invent."[54]

The debate on whether women write differently is ongoing and no conclusive evidence on the issue has been presented by feminist critics. Most of the hypotheses based on the gender of the writer and that of the text need more stylistic studies to be substantiated. The writings on this subject verge on wishful thinking and have not reached

---

51 See this volume p. 124.
52 Susan Stanford Friedman, "Women's autobiographical selves: theory and practice" in Shari Benstock (ed.), *The Private Self: Theory and Practice of Women's Autobiographical Writings* (London, Routledge, 1988), p. 39.
53 Ibid., p. 55.
54 See this volume p. 44.

the stage where they can be considered as theories. Nevertheless, the following is a summary of the debates on "women's" writing.

Nancy Chodorow, the revisionist psychoanalytic theorist, suggests that the process of individuation differs for men and women: "The girl comes to speak tentatively from outside the prevailing framework of individuality: she brings a different kind of voice to her narrative."[55] Women speak loudly in a different voice and an alternative "language of fluid, plural subjectivity". As a result women have a distinct and gender-specific identity which reflects itself in the texts of their autobiographies.

But how does the language of plural subjectivity subvert and disrupt the man-made language which brings with it a pre-existing order? "Language accumulates an ineluctable memory which does not even know itself as memory. Men believe that language is their servant and do not realise that language has a memory of its own and historical dimensions practitioners are unaware of."[56] That memory traces the history of male victories and achievement within which the feminine is repressed. That feminine is what women writers articulate in a language closely bound with the body.

Luce Irigarary and Hélène Cixous have identified a difference between men and women in their use of language. It is a mode of speech and writing which Irigarary calls "womenspeak" and Hélène Cixous calls "écriture feminine". By writing herself in the discourse of women, the woman writer will return to the body, and language becomes closely bound to sexuality.[57]

"Feminine" writing is "plural, continuous, interdependent, non-sensical, roundabout, a narrative of ruptures, gaps, wordplay, and

---

55 Sidonie Smith, *A Poetics of Women's Autobiography: Marginality and the Fictions of Self-Representation* (Bloomington, Indiana University Press, 1987), p. 12.

56 Michel Foucault, *The Order of Things: an Archaeology of the Human Sciences* (London, Tavistock Publications, 1970), p. 297.

57 Catherine Belsey and Jane Moore (eds.), *The Feminist Reader: Essays in Gender and the Politics of Literary Criticism* (London, Macmillan, 1989), p. 14.

jouissance fundamentally different from the forward drive of logocentric certitude and individuality."[58] This *jouissance* signals the unknowable and unrepresentable, the "feminine". But later on Cixous modifies her original argument and states that "feminine writing" is not determined by the sex of the author; it is only signified by the gender of the text. So this type of "narrative" could be produced by women or men and it thrives in an androgynous, genderless space.

The writing of Hoda Barakat was considered by the critics as genderless. This implies, within an Arab context, a woman writer who has broken away from "female" identity and writing, which is perceived as the inferior narrative of the first person, romantic fiction and infantile style. In *The Stone of Laughter*[59] Barakat consciously attempts to subvert the Arabic language with full awareness of its memory and gender: "Perhaps what I mean is that when I write I step outside my gender, outside any gender."[60]

The language used by the women writers who contributed to this anthology could be best described or "explained" by what Marguerite Duras said in 1975: "I think 'feminine literature' is an organic, translated writing . . . translated from blackness, from darkness. Women have been in darkness for centuries. And when women write, they translate this darkness."[61] She goes on to add that it is like a new way of communicating, rather than an already formed language.

In the Arab world the already formed language is not only one language but is divided into many sub-languages. "One of the most striking characteristics of what we call classical Arabic (*fusha*) is the radical dichotomy it presupposes between everyday colloquial

---

58 Sidonie Smith, *A Poetics of Women's Autobiography: Marginality and the Fictions of Self-Representation* (Bloomington, Indiana University Press, 1987), p. 13.
59 Hoda Barakat, *The Stone of Laughter* (Reading, Garnet Publishing, 1995).
60 See this volume p. 45.
61 Elaine Marks and Isabelle de Courtivron, *New French Feminism: an Anthology* (London, Harvester Wheatseaf, 1981), p. 174.

and formal language."[62] This rift has reinforced traditional social divisions between those who use the classical language, with its rigid structure and religious roots, and those who articulate their daily experiences in a language which is neither classical nor colloquial and in some cases close to the oral or folk culture. Women belong to the second group, whose subjectivity and daily experiences are not articulated by the classical Arabic of the establishment.

The task of women writers, therefore, becomes extremely complicated and instead of effecting a single translation, they have to carry out a multiple translation of the darkness, espoused with a search for a new language free of the religious and dominant. They articulate the special vision of their experience into linear Arabic, creating at the same time a tradition of self-representation for women within the Arab culture, and possibly a new language. Although still searching and formulating this new language, Arab women might succeed in challenging what Sharabi describes as "the monological culture . . . that commands and legislates their [the poor, the young and women] life from above."[63]

Forty years ago, women's writing in the Arab world began attracting attention with the publication of Layla Ba'lbaki's *Ana Ahya*. Since then the writings of Hoda Barakat, Alia Mamdouh, Salwa Bakr, Liana Badr, Hanan el-Sheikh, Radwa Ashour, Hadia Said, 'Alya' al-Tabi'i, Ghada al-Samman, Sahar Khalifa and many others have been published throughout the Arab world. But it is still too early to decide whether Arab women write differently from Arab men, and whether there is a definitive female style. Probably women writers have carved a place for themselves within the Arabic language, but this is a relatively recent phenomenon and needs to be studied and analysed further. What is certain at this juncture is that Arab women will turn more and more to the genre of autobiography to explore, articulate and promote themselves; it will take a long time for the "master narrative" of

---

62 Hisham Sharabi, *Neopatriarchy: a Theory of Distorted Change in Arab Society* (Oxford, Oxford University Press, 1988), p. 84.
63 Ibid., p. 89.

neopatriarchy to be challenged and disrupted, and for Arab women to weave a "language" of their own, thus freeing the forces of modernisation in Arab societies.

LIANA BADR

Liana Badr was born in 1952 in Palestinian Jerusalem. She left for Jordan in 1967 with her father, where she began her studies at the University of Jordan. She was unable to complete her education, as she was forced to leave Jordan in 1970 because of Black September.

Badr, like many other Palestinians of the diaspora, has resided in Beirut, Damascus and Tunis.

Her first novel, *A Compass for the Sunflower* (Busala Li 'Abbad ash-Shams) was published in 1979. She has also written a number of stories for children and three collections of short stories: *Qisas al-Hub wa-l-Mulahaqa* (Stories of Love and Pursuit), 1983, *A Balcony Over Fakahani* (Nafidha 'ala al-Fakahani), 1983 and *Ana Auriyd an-Nahar* (I Want the Day), 1985. More recently she has published two further novels *Nujum Ariha* (The Stars of Jericho), 1993 and *'Ayn al-Mira'a* (The Eye of the Mirror) which was published in English by Garnet in 1995. She now lives in Jericho where she is at present the head of the Audio-Visual Department at the Palestinian Ministry of Culture.

THE STORY OF A NOVEL OR
REFLECTIONS OF DETAILS IN THE MIRROR:
BETWEEN AWARENESS AND MADNESS

LIANA BADR

⸎

When I was in the first years of flowering, my mother warned me against standing for too long in front of the mirror. She elaborated her point by explaining that desire is a dangerous thing for a girl in our society, as is exploring the coverings which shield the body from the eyes and words of others that can so easily enclose it in their grasp. But above all, she wanted to protect me from the eye of the mirror because it is the eye of eyes, the one which sows destruction through its numerous reflections and infinite layers. Heaven itself may be composed of seven layers, yet no one knows how deep is the well of the smooth and shiny mirror. Its cold eye has stared relentlessly at human beings and their bodies since time immemorial and, more dangerously, it has stared at their souls as well. With untiring tenderness my mother forbade me from going near that evil glass which invariably undertakes a dialogue with the soul. For how can you communicate with yourself if not through some sort of mirror? And where else can you yield to the demands of your conscience? The mirror has a deadly charm which penetrates deep inside a person, tempting you to look at yourself and examine how you relate to the world, pushing you to the edge of insanity. How often did she tell me – can you stare at the sun for long without being blinded, without damaging your sight? At that time it was not in my grasp to judge or consider more carefully what I was being told.

But later, the many wars which I lived through compelled me to undertake a careful examination and to try to steal some of the divine fire of knowledge which flames in the daytime sun and which human beings can only trap by means of their cold, metallic mirrors. When the fire was stolen from the gods by Prometheus, the mirror represented the irresistible temptation of infinite knowledge to which human beings have no right within our culture and tradition.

But from early childhood and for many years afterwards, I dared not look into the mirror except from time to time to glance at some detail of my appearance. The glances were brief and fleeting even though I was then living in Beirut, the place where it takes a long time to settle in exile. During the ten years I spent there, every sheet of silvery glass reflected anxiety, corroded existence and that fear which attacks from within you. After the loss imposed upon us by the departure to Beirut following the clashes of Black September in Jordan and the shock of relocating to a completely new land, the city was only a trembling image mirroring our search for ourselves. How would we find our way among dozens of movements and directions, hundreds of conflicts and confrontations? And how could one contemplate introspection in a town that deprived its inhabitants of work permits, factional privileges, even the joy of being a tourist?

In Shatilla refugee camp I worked with women as a voluntary social worker. It was there that I began to see the many fissures the Palestinians of the diaspora had in common: uprootedness; segregation within a city replete with drugs; the confiscation and pillage; the misery of bereavement and the loss of property. These were some of the many elements which formed the basis of exile and enforced migration. With and amongst the women began the endless flow of stories, from morning till night, wonderfully plaited into a sunny strand – Um Kamal telling of eternal longing, always ready to burst; Widad joking and laughing despite the worry of feeding eight children; Um Khalil, whose children were killed nearly ten years later in the massacres of Sabra and Shatilla; Salma, whose mother was killed by army snipers at the camp during the events of May 1973, and Salwa, whose nose was broken because her husband did not find a hot dinner on his return. People's tales, their individual flavours and their misery erupt but fail to deprive them of their *joie de vivre* which can be seen in small rituals whose significance is well understood by the women. They would spray water on the threshold of the houses, praising the day when the camp was granted autonomy, in spite of knowing that in the past severe fines were imposed on everyone who sprayed water in front of the house. All this was a large mirror reflecting a world which I began to discover by learning about the different Palestinian communities. For I am a daughter of the West Bank who was not able to get to know the Palestinians of Galilee because of the 1948 occupation. I began to understand the Palestinians of the diaspora the day I began to observe the many factors we had in common and that united us as one people. Of course there were striking differences in the lifestyles between the Palestinians residing in the Gulf and those who had settled elsewhere; different places accounted for a variety of tastes and living standards, and yet there was unity in the existential sense, a unity expressed in the search for a cultural identity and a self, despite dispersal. All this did not take place in Baqa refugee camp in Jordan where, as students, we volunteered for social work, nor at home (my birthplace) in Jerusalem, nor in the city where I and my heart lived, Jericho. It happened in Lebanon where, together with the Palestinians from Galilee, I celebrated the discovery of myself and the relationship with Palestine in a new way, one that broke from the straight line that divided everything into one side or the other. Up close I began to see what I had not seen before.

At the outbreak of the civil war in Lebanon, looking in the mirror was no longer possible because, engrossed in my struggle for survival, I had turned from the inner world of a confused self for whom the glass hanging on the wall had become completely out of reach. How could you meditate or find time for yourself among bombshells and gunfire, when water, provisions, as well as your basic security were lost? And you turned away from mirrors since it did not occur that they should be viewed as anything other than time bombs ready to splinter and shatter with the next explosion. During the many years of civil war I did not approach a window or a mirror without an overwhelming feeling of insecurity because of the harm latent in them. The glass would break, the mirror shatter and the cement crumble. The only indestructible thing left in life was everybody's obsessive will to survive.

After leaving Beirut I was overcome by extended paroxysms of weeping the likes of which I had not known before. I began looking at mirrors trying to understand what we couldn't get used to, to get a taste of the new exile which we hadn't predicted.

I started staring into that piece of shiny glass which until then had scared me away, scrutinising my swollen eyelids, searching for traces of repressed tears or bouts of sleeplessness. To what world tossed on heaving seas had we been taken? After the massacre of Sabra and Shatilla, when the war of the camps was breaking out, I had reached a point when I felt the inescapable need to confront the mirror. Why were my people the victims of such hatred and such methods of annihilation? What had we done? Were we being punished for rejecting compliance and dissolution, for wanting to recover an identity meaningful to us and a homeland of which we knew nothing except that we were not there? Why were our lives a succession of absences and how could we try to prove our existence when the only means we possessed were transitory and illusory?

It distressed me that one or two of our camps were, from time to time, faced with systematic destruction, and I began to wonder if each time wasn't simply a repetition of Tal el-Za'tar. Do people think that the silence which followed the clamour after each genocide is normal? Is it not time for us to begin the war of memory to fight to preserve what happened to us after the dispersal from the homeland? Is it not up to us to build everything that was lost or fragmented?

In 1984 I began my meticulous study of the story of Tal el-Za'tar which became immortalised during those days of steadfastness. For the young girl and the woman, the elderly man and the fighter, those days are still with them. Words began to pour out, images to form, songs to ring out, tales and proverbs to be recalled, endlessly flowing out in the aftermath of terror. We began to relive the events, exchange stories, follow up fates and search for those missing. There was no longer any Palestine, neither state nor country, but it was re-created out of the details told by those who lived through the annihilation. A burning quest for knowledge of what had happened tormented me. The people of Tal el-Za'tar spared me nothing. Even the emaciated maps which I used to draw as support to my few recollections were corrected by their tales and their descriptions. I would delve into their memories with the same vehemence with which I gathered facts about military patrols, types of shells and sandbags. I wanted to know about the ingenious ways they found to secure food, clothing and protection. They lavished details on me which I scrutinised and compared, and from which I deduced and reconstructed the missing bits. I disentangled the interwoven facts, allowing the centre of the circle to appear amidst the dust. I escaped from the misery of endings to the joy of continuity. All this is not just a large mirror reflecting power, challenge and sacrifices, but it is also a song of love of life and human beings, a passionate hymn to living, enabling us as humans to learn the secret of survival on Earth despite the initial predatory monsters, and the now continual and devastating wars. When I wrote *The Eye of the Mirror* I was writing a profound love story between people and nature, between people and people. There, in the fire of disaster, discrimination and disintegration, all that remained were long hours of effort devoted to the attempt to protect others. In the story of Tal el-Za'tar I found another face, one contrasting with the horrors of war, one radiating spontaneity, solidarity and steadfastness, the roots of the collective sentiments with which the Palestinians held on to their memory and identity.

Yet, in the novel, the mirror becomes a splinter that wounds Aisha's hand so that it bleeds. There is no attaining of self-awareness other than by transcending the limits of pain and madness. When I was writing the chapter about the exodus from the camp and the killings that took place, children and adolescents were falling in the streets during the Palestinian *intifada* for no reason other than their devotion to a homeland. A novel is not merely a mirror hanging along a road, as Stendhal said. I have not found that the mirror has its own life nor that it has any self or soul except when I worked on the story of Tal el-Za'tar and witnessed the astounding tenacity of the camp. Yes, a person may lose his mind when seeing death and destruction all around him. But isn't the mirror a world opposite the world, one that gives us an immense capability for struggling, wrestling and facing challenges? Also, isn't the mirror a world in itself which makes us doubt the validity of its reflections when these are not tied to action and commitment?

In any case, each of us has his own mirror, but our collective mirror is one which shares in the shaping of our existence or in the spreading of misery. That is not all. More importantly, are we always up to following the road the mirror casts ahead of us and maintaining a lucidity resembling delirium, as we acquire a knowledge which hammers on the door of madness? This is what I tried to do in *The Eye of the Mirror*, a book which was written by the lives of the people of the camp before ink traced the lines and letters.

Salwa Bakr

Salwa Bakr was born in Cairo in 1949, the daughter of a railway worker. She gained her BA in Business Management from 'Ayn Shams University in 1972 but this did not fulfil her academic interests and hence four years later she graduated with a second BA, this time in drama criticism. She then went on to graduate study in history and literary criticism.

She began writing in the mid-1970s, and her work has been met with much critical acclaim. *Zinat fi Janazat ar-Ra'is* (Zinat at the President's Funeral), 1985, Bakr's first collection of short stories, was published at her own expense, but its success ensured that she had no difficulties finding publishers for her other collections, *Maqam 'Atiyya* (The Shrine of Atia), 1986, *'An il-Ruh al-lati Suriqat Tadrijiyyan* (On the Gradually Departing Spirit), 1989, and *Ajin al-Fallaha* (The Peasant Woman's Dough), 1992.

Bakr lived for several years in Cyprus with her husband, where she worked as a film critic for a number of Arabic-language publications, before returning to Egypt in 1986, where she has since been concentrating on her creative writing. Other pieces of Bakr's work, published in English, in addition to "Writing as a way out", can be found in

My Grandmother's Cactus (1993) and *The Wiles of Men* (1992). The second of her novels, *The Golden Chariot* (al-'Araba al-dhahabiyya la Tas'ad ila-l-Sama') was published by Garnet Publishing in 1995.

Her latest novel, *Wasf al-Bulbul* (Describing the Nightingale), was published in 1993.

Bakr's life and work have been greatly affected by the 1967 Six-Day War defeat of Egypt by Israel – an event which she herself described as the first of many defeats. The repression in all spheres of Egyptian life and in particular the political sphere is perhaps Bakr's greatest concern. However, she maintains that both men and women can be liberated through the contributions of women's writings.

WRITING AS A WAY OUT

SALWA BAKR

Until the age of about thirty, I was submerged in illusions – illusions of politics and illusions of men.

When the revolution of July 1952[1] took place, I was no more than three years old. Three years later I started school, my plaits tied and decorated with ribbons in the colours of the flag of the new revolution. The first songs of my childhood were in support of the revolution and against colonialism, oppression and injustice.

By the end of my primary education, I had learned to march in demonstrations, demonstrations in support of Algerian liberation from French colonialism, demonstrations against Abd al-Karim Qasim in Iraq, demonstrations protesting against the fate of the Zaïrean hero, Lumumba. By the time I graduated from university, the political police had a file on me, describing me as an extreme leftist who could be detained at any time. This eventually happened in 1989 when I was held in prison for two weeks accused of inciting the workers of the

---

1 The 23 July 1952 saw the start of the Free Officers' rising against the King and the old regime.

iron and steel works in Helwan to go on strike – an event that did not actually happen. I was released and no charge was brought against me, this time.

As for men, I was brought up like millions of girls of my generation, with the idea that I had no existence without a man, the basic desire in life of every girl. Thus she must be beautiful, gentle and elegant for the sake of a man. Even education was placed in the context of giving me added value, so as to draw admiration from and bring pleasure to one sole being – man.

Thus thirty years of my life were wasted, until I discovered the falseness of politics and the illusion of man.

My illusions about men were dispelled after many failed emotional experiences, some of which culminated in my entering into the institution of marriage. Naturally, I plunged into relationships with intellectual men or those preoccupied with politics who spoke at length about human justice and fraternity and the necessity of eliminating the oppression of one human being by another.

But what of women, my good sirs? In theory, the talk was about the necessity of fighting class and sexual subjugation. However, in reality and in everyday practice, it was I who had to cook, wash, clean, and look after household affairs, I who had to maintain traditions and values, not to smoke, not raise my voice, but behave like any other woman maintaining traditions and taking care to display the traditional image of marital relations to other people, so that it could not be said that radical progressives were permissive, immoral, or that their women were loose. I had to do even more than ordinary women so as to set an example. So I did not adorn myself or ever behave coarsely. Thus I was able to please all parties – intellectual, thinking men and ordinary, trivial men.

That was my image, like that of thousands of girls of my generation who were subjected to this kind of experience and who fell under the influence of illusions.

While uncovering the greatest illusion of all, concerning men, I also discovered my political illusions. Day by day, the great theories proved to be failures and out of touch with reality. Those groups of amateur politicians who supported them shifted from a Stalinist position to a Maoist or Trotskyist position with ease, without moving from their seats. This was apart from those who finally left our country and withdrew to oil-producing countries, acquired the benefits of the black gold and resumed the pattern of their lives away from politics and the great slogans which nevertheless they frequently continued to proclaim.

Many women fell victim to this political illusion and ended up with psychological problems – they drifted towards madness, attempted suicide or, in cases of extreme retreat of values, put on the veil and hid behind the doors of their houses and, like all traditional women, bore backward values and norms on our behalf.

I lived long periods of loss – I experienced loss of hope, feelings of worthlessness and the sense that I was not standing on real, solid ground. I was deprived of security and safety, until I discovered writing as a way out for myself.

At the start, writing was my true saviour, through which I was able to express my repressed feelings, my anger and my views on the life which I had lived and was living. But with time, I found that writing was my real existence, that it was far from being merely a way to vent my repressed feelings. It was the real impulse that protected me from either madness or suicide. Thus writing presented me with a golden opportunity to be myself, outside the frameworks, the institutions, the customary system of values and norms. Within the space of the white page, I could construct my chosen religion, my own morality, my desired politics, my better world. Here I am really free, away from the illusory past and the nightmare present.

For me, creative writing demolished many idols I used to worship and honour – preconceived ideas, the claim to absolute interpretation of the world and of life – for nothing is as it seems, no truth unchangeable. The more I discover this, the more I master free writing, liberated not only from moulds and fabrications, but free to concentrate on humanity in all its forms, concerning myself with marginalised and crushed human beings whom nobody seems to care about.

Perhaps it was from this perspective that my concentration on women developed. I do not wish to place myself in a defined mould; I disagree with labels, and am against classification, but I am a woman who has suffered greatly simply for being a woman and feel acutely the suffering of women like myself. My knowledge of women and their concerns is thus an intimate one. For this reason I write about women first and foremost, even though entering into the world of writing did not ease my suffering as a woman, for my battle became clear as a woman writer, a woman who emerged from the customary and normal context of a society. I chose an alternative path to that of being a means of reproduction, a vessel for pregnancy. Nobody in the social environment in which a woman writer lives treats her as a creative writer with a distinct and different world. The first and traditional way of treating a woman is the prevalent way of treating women writers. More importantly, criticism often makes light of what women write. It is true that I have received critical acclaim since the publication of my first collection of short stories, *Zinat fi Janazat ar-Ra'is* (Zinat at the President's Funeral), but this reception was tinged with caution, for male critics often avoid dealing with women writers for "moral" reasons and for fear of being accused of having ulterior motives behind their attention to these writers; thus female critics often wrote about my writing.

From another perspective, male criticism does not pay attention to women's distinctive creativity; neither, for naturally pragmatic reasons, does it consider a woman's specific talents for storytelling, language, and portrayal of character. Women's creativity is seen, first and foremost, through male eyes.

The woman writer also suffers from the attempt to invent a congruence between the world of the characters which she creates and her own personality. Every story I have written has been assumed by some to be my personal story, this notion stifles creativity. In addition there are the three taboos which the woman writer usually fears approaching – religion, sex and politics.

But in any case, I pay the tax for courage, confrontation and resistance; above all, I have to pay the tax for being a woman writer.

It is a heavy tax on many levels, especially in a society in which most individuals are illiterate, a society which is conservative by nature, whose values are static and which does not respect women in the first place. All this makes writing seem like the task of Sisyphus, particularly if the writer stops to wonder for whom she is writing. But this does not stand as an obstacle between myself and writing because I have chosen it as a path to knowledge, liberation, and discovery of the world and myself.

HODA BARAKAT

Hoda Barakat was born in Beirut in 1952. In 1974 she was awarded a degree in French Literature by the Lebanese University in Beirut; she then taught for a year in the village of al-Khaim in the south of Lebanon. With the outbreak of civil war in 1975, Barakat moved to Bshari, a village in the north of Lebanon.

In 1975 she went to Paris to start a Ph.D., but because of the civil war she returned to Lebanon after one year and worked as a teacher, journalist and translator. Her first collection of short stories, *Za'irat* (Women Visitors), was published in 1985. From 1985 to 1986, Barakat worked at the Centre for Lebanese Research, Beirut. In 1988, she helped establish *Shahrazad*, a women's magazine. Her first novel, *Hajar al-Dahik* (*The Stone of Laughter*), written in Lebanon during the civil war, received the Al-Naqid Literary Prize for First Novels. *The Stone of Laughter* was later translated into French, English and Italian. Her second novel, *Ahl el-Hawa* (People of Love), was published in 1993.

Hoda Barakat has lived and worked in Paris since 1989.

I WRITE AGAINST MY HAND

HODA BARAKAT

ৼৡৣৡৡৄ

Whenever I think of that odd activity – writing – it seems to me that it is both profoundly ambiguous and peculiarly equivocal.

What modesty to write, but also, what presumption, what arrogance! Each piece of writing – in its despair and desolation – resembles those messages placed in glass bottles and thrown into the sea. When the world is cut off from us, it feigns ignorance of our writing. When my voice is no longer heard and my eyes are unable to see, then, I say, nothing remains but absence and my world breaks down. Let those who have no need or time for me go in peace. I give them complete freedom to read me or leave me. Therefore I offer the one who chooses to read me the very same thing I give myself, a surrender only to the demands of words.

We are so humble that we disappear. But we also disappear because the one face to face with us is not up to reaching us; we disappear so that our writing can shine through all the stronger, because it takes so long for our presence to be acknowledged. We know very well that when we raise the spoken word to the level of written language, we are treating it as sacred and trying to preserve its imprint in collective memory and history.

The purpose of all writing is truth. It purports to discover a truth not previously recorded; it purports to deliver prophecy and authority.

We do not write unless we are alone, as desolate and spurned as a man who is dying. We write only in silence and solitude. Alone with the hand that we use. Alone with ourselves, with the hollowness of things, with what remains when we have stripped the world around us. We write to multiply and become universal, to become condensed and to expand, to multiply and to become one, because we want to be the totality.

In all writing there is much generalising and a tendency to talk over people's heads. We withdraw from this world, aggrieved, and then come back as priests, messengers and rulers. As our books are printed and reprinted, we are filled with vanity and joy derived from a world that does not deserve to be addressed.

We write, I write, from a dual perspective, because I am a woman and want to resemble a man, to cut short the time for training and amateurism, and prove my intellectual ability to construct and to invent. In order to make my reader forget that I am *qasir*, a minor, I have sometimes toyed with the idea of writing under a male pseudonym. Let me mention here a very well-known critic who wrote an article about my novel, *The Stone of Laughter*, in one of the most widely sold Arab newspapers. He praised it in a way that meant that although I was a woman I had succeeded in writing a good novel and had not sunk to the level of the mechanical writing of feminists.

I also write because I am a woman who cannot be anything other, and as someone who does not want to resemble men at all. I know that I am different and that I have my own sensibility, and I embrace these facts gladly.

And I write also because I want to resemble no person or thing, but to go deeper within myself, to resemble myself and coincide with myself. Perhaps what I mean is that when I write I step outside my gender, outside any gender. It seems to me that the act of writing is out of the ordinary, beyond the conditioning and characteristics of male and female social behaviour. Or it is at the junction of this restrictive division into male and female and full of the elation arising from the blending of the genders and the resulting ambiguity. It may be that the essence of creative writing lies in that merging of the sexes, the one with the other, which occurs among plants that exchange their pollen in the peace and harmony of open spaces. Writing also requires absolute ignorance of its sources, of its gender and of any frame of reference and it goes against any claim to reduce it to a mere profession. But it also results from a clear vision of both the source and estuary of the river – in other words, the motive and goal of writing – so that it does not become just symbols, empty composition, rhetoric and unadulterated ideology.

When we write we are both male and female and yet at the same time well beyond either.

I write, we write to avenge ourselves against the world. At the beginning, we wrote on the walls of caves. Because my neighbour lent me grain, I drew pictures of grains when the rain fell, writing it down to remind myself that I owed him something I must return. We continue to write for the same reasons. Because the world owes us things which are not recognised or not remembered, we write so that the world can regain its memory, so that we can collect its debt. We write to recover the things which are ours and which the world denies us. We write to retrieve and to take revenge.

But we also write to leave everything to the wind, to allow ourselves to drift, in want of nothing. We write to say that we have nothing and that we are but fine particles of dust to be scattered by the first gust of wind. We are in the same pigeon-hole as those exposing their body and belongings to scribes and seers, to negation, we risk being confined to the margin and regarded as of no consequence. We write to belong to the disinherited, to the simple souls who own nothing except speech and its rumble, and who live in its paper house. We write so that we can stand on our own two feet.

We write because we are useless, because we do not make bread like the baker, provide water like the plumber or erect houses like the builder. We write because nobody needs us, because there is no reward for writing. Because we do not have fathers who summon us to dinner in the evening after the weariness of the field. Because we are not people of toil nor sowers of seeds. Because we are cicada. But we write about the glory of cicada and the songs of the forest, about the illusion of summer, about skies clearing, about space. We write to feed the ant its grain and let it enjoy it. And if we stay on the outskirts, it is because we claim that there is no text without us. We write to be real and to persist.

We write, I write in wars and civil wars because I have no power, no strength, no weapons and no soldiers. I write because I crouch in the cellar like a rat, raising my cowardice like a child in times of hardship. I belong to the dark dampness and the forgetfulness of those who have placed history in the streets. But I also write as the rat that gnaws at foundations and pillars. I betray the establishment and give evidence against it. I write beneath the boots which stamp on my face, as if *I* were the emperor or the dictator.

I write for myself and against myself, against my tribe and my memory, against my grandfather and my father so that I can bury them and remember them well. I write for the void, for forgetfulness, because I have chosen the proof – memory. I write because I am free, because I can never be free.

Sometimes I write against what my eyes witness.

And I write against my hand.

FADIA FAQIR

Fadia Faqir was born in Amman, Jordan. She gained her BA in English Literature from the University of Jordan, Amman, before undertaking an MA in creative writing at Lancaster University. She completed her Ph.D. in creative writing at the University of East Anglia.

Her first novel, *Nisanit* was published by Viking/Penguin in 1990. *Pillars of Salt*, her second novel was published by Quartet, it has also been translated into German and Dutch.

Faqir is general editor of the award-winning Arab Women Writers series published by Garnet Publishing and is also a lecturer and co-ordinator for the Project of Middle Eastern Women's Studies at the Centre for Middle Eastern and Islamic Studies University of Durham.

STORIES FROM THE HOUSE
OF SONGS

FADIA FAQIR

There was, there was not, at the oldest of times a country which extended from the Persian Gulf to the Atlantic ocean. In that country, which I shall call Baghdad for the purposes of this narrative, Islam was the predominant religion. Islam, or that particular interpretation of the *hadith* and Qur'an, perceives a specific role for women which in practice places them at the bottom of the social hierarchy – "men are superior to them by a degree".[1] Islam identified women with chaos, anti-divine and anti-social forces. To contain women's power, a system of segregation and confinement was superimposed on the many and diverse societies in Baghdad. The unchecked rights of men, polygamy and divorce, were all strategies to subjugate women. A true Islamic Baghdadi house was a house where men provided for women, protected women and policed them.

---

1 The Qur'an, Surat "Al-Nisa".

51

There was a storyteller in Baghdad called Shahrazad. Committing her life to telling tales in such hostile surroundings, she entered into a conflict with the religious and political orders. Becoming a woman writer in Baghdad was to face a double challenge as there was a consensus in that land that denied woman a voice. Although writing in Baghdad was not a respectable profession and was considered by the men of religion to be an act of subversion, many women, like Shahrazad, chose writing as a means to freedom by taking sides in the social and political struggle. But these women were writing in societies which forbade any discussion of sex, religion and politics in the classroom. As a consequence, they experienced slander, prohibition and imprisonment. To cross the defined border and encroach on traditionally male space was to risk being accused of being a loose woman, a whore, a belly-dancer. In most Baghdadi countries, women's writing was read as autobiographical. Many women writers, among them Layla Ba'lbaki, Zabia Khamis, Suhair el-Tal, Nawal el-Saadawi, were held legally responsible for their creations.

Shahrazad suffered the consequences of living as a woman in a conservative Muslim society. When she became a reporter with a local newspaper, she was asked to cover "women's stuff". When she moved on to other areas like politics and economics, many of her articles were censored. Political, social and religious censorship was the Baghdadis' daily nightmare – their strait-jacket. Commenting on the question of freedom, Margaret Walker writes, "Without freedom, personal and social, to write as one pleases . . . the writer is in bondage."[2] In Baghdad Shahrazad had no social, religious or political freedom – she was in bondage. Returning to the house of obedience before sunset prayers, she was forced to wear the veil and could not criticise the regime.

Shahrazad would shake her stick at what Ian McEwan describes as the "monochrome, the monological, the monotheoretical, the monotheistic".[3] When faith is presented as all or nothing, when two

---

2 Margaret Walker, "On being female, black and free" in *The Writer and Her Work*, ed., Janet Sternberg (New York, W. W. Norton, 1980).

3 Ian McEwan, *New Statesman and Society*, 3 March 1989.

plus two no longer equals four, when singing is no longer a means of deliverance, the writer must decide to follow the men of religion, to be a clown of the court, or to write the truth of her heart. Shahrazad wanted to safeguard her integrity, and the purity of her tales. She wanted to look at her face in the mirror without seeing an ever-running, red tear. She wanted freedom, to teach her children songs of peace, so she left Baghdad. She refused to let her song be silenced or distorted. She would sing loud and clear and so she crossed from one language into another, committing herself to a life in exile.

Exile is a sad country. In exile the rift between the rural image of the homeland and the western city cannot be healed. It is a severing from home, Eden, childhood; it is a sense of loss, displacement, uprootedness. In exile, nostalgia becomes a form of loyalty to the house in Baghdad, to the garden with its tall palm trees, to the mother's headscarf, to the past, the village; all are images held still in a medium which beautifies.

In exile, you quickly develop a double vision, where images of the streets of Basra merge with those of Kentish Town. You begin looking forward at the country of adoption while always looking back at the country of origin. You check your position at every junction. You adjust your mirrors, your sense of belonging, and drive on exploring a new map. You keep examining and re-examining your loyalties to both the still picture in the mind and the present living landscape. You no longer take things at face value. Doubt, dissent and questioning become part of your life. You become a hybrid, forever assessing, evaluating, accommodating.

Exile is a sad country. The first cultural shock comes when you fail to recognise the truth of your experience in the Western perception of it. You feel out-numbered and out-organised by a culture which validates and enforces the supremacy of everything that is Christian, Western, white, written. At the least provocation, distaste for immigrant culture comes to the surface. What you have left behind in your country of origin becomes clear – dictatorship, fundamentalism and the mutilation of the mind. But you cannot fight the authoritarian sultans and mullahs without fighting reductionism, colonialism and misrepresentation in the Western media. In your country of adoption you suddenly realise that – to use the words of Fred Halliday – you have to "turn a critical face both ways, towards the country of origin and its traditions and the country of reception. The challenge, the alienation, the 'offence' are two-sided."[4]

In this multicultural, multiracial society Shahrazad, the daughter of the vizier, became an émigré wrapped in her raincoat, untouchable, without background or history. She stood outside the circle with the "miscellaneous whining coloured" who are denied access to the circle where, as Edward Said writes, "stand the blameless, the just, the omnicompetent, those who know the truth about themselves as well as others".[5] She began asking herself: Who am I? Where do I belong? Where is my fatherland? What is my mother tongue? To whom should I tell my tales?

When she first arrived in her country of adoption, she was given a simple answer to her questions – the cricket match test. After filling in endless forms as the immigration officer checked the reams of blacklists, she was asked, "If we play cricket against Baghdad, which team would you support?" She found no words in any language to answer his question. She stood there opening and shutting her mouth like a fish. Would they open her up? Probe into her immigrant's heart and see what was etched there? The house of obedience which Shahrazad had left behind rose again as the house of confinement.

The real test for Shahrazad came the year of Desert Storm. This was not cricket – her country of adoption began a war against Baghdad. Day after day she watched the bombs falling on her people. Some of her Baghdadi friends who had escaped the sultan's secret police were detained and imprisoned. Other Baghdadis, who had lost members of their families, had to go through the agony of watching the Western media coverage of the war. Baghdad was destroyed but

---

4 Fred Halliday, "The struggle for the migrant soul", *The Times Literary Supplement*, 14-20 April 1989.
5 Edward Said, "Reflections on exile", *Granta 13*, Autumn 1984.

the sultan lived on. This operation, launched in the name of "law and order", left nothing but disorder and destruction.

Are there any bandages for the eyes, the ears and the heart? The casualties along the Basra road were buried in the sand – almost a generation of Baghdadis was "neutralised", many of them peasant boys coerced into conscription. The poet Tony Harrison writes:

> So lie and say the charred man smiled
> to see the soldier hug his child
> This gaping rictus once made glad
> a few old hearts back in Baghdad
> hearts growing older by the minute
> as each truck comes without me in it[6]

Shahrazad had met the "old hearts back in Baghdad". For her they have faces, they have names. She sings their songs, understands their sadness, laughs at their jokes. But they said they would kill them and they did – the soldiers' bodies on the Basra road – but the old hearts remain.

She tried in the name of understanding and assimilation to join the majority of the public who gave their stamp of approval to Desert Storm. But there was another wind, blowing strongly from Basra, carrying the smell of ripe dates and the memory of her mother's patient eyes. She could not join the chorus of those who said "I love you" to the war machine. Shahrazad, the storyteller, the daughter of the vizier, became an embittered émigré. She buttoned up her raincoat, standing in silence on the outside. The walls of the house of confinement were closing in. Exile stops being a rift and becomes a wound. Mahmoud Darwish describes this state of siege:

> Out of the window of this last space.
> Our star will hang up mirrors.

---

6 Tony Harrison, "A Cold Coming", the *Guardian*, 18 March, 1991.

Where should we go after the last frontiers?
Where should the birds fly after the last sky?[7]

She vowed to tie her tongue with the same yellow ribbons that were
tied round the old oak tree to welcome the allied forces back home.
May this tongue never utter another word in English, the language
of her coloniser and invader. The English language is contaminated,
corrupt, full of "neutralising", "terminating", "taking apart", "knocking
out" and "cleansing" hostile targets. Shahrazad felt betrayed by her
first love – the English language. It was no longer the clear, sharp,
crisp language which she had pursued the way her bedouin ancestors
used to pursue fresh water.

She remembered the language she had fallen in love with when she
was young. Her first experience of the English language in secondary
school was memorising Shakespeare's poems and listening to the
radio. One of the things she had to do to join the secret Society,
a local adolescent group, was memorise English songs. She learnt
by heart 'Love Story' and 'Nights in White Satin', put on a tee shirt,
worn-out jeans, pinned the sign of peace on her chest, put a flower
in her hair then – yeah man – was given membership. She sang in
English, "Imagine there's no countries."

"May my tongue never utter another word of English," she said.
She wanted to follow Ngugi's example – "to resolve the question
of language, which was clearly inseparable from the question of to
which tradition I would reconnect myself."[8] In his defiance of the
intended detention of his mind and imagination he decided to write
in Gikuyu. He argues that the colonial system imposes its own
language on subject races and then the acquisition of their tongue
becomes a status symbol. The alienation from the mother tongue,
and adoption of the thought process and values of the colonial
system distance you from the masses of your country. Ngugi decided

---

7 Mahmoud Darwish, "The earth is closing on us", trs. Abdullah al-Udhari,
   in *Victims of a Map* (London, Al Saqi Books, 1984), p. 13.
8 Ngugi Wa Thiong'o, "The language of African fiction", in *Decolonising
   the Mind* (London, Heinemann, 1986).

to communicate with the people he left behind in Gikuyu, the language of his new commitment.

Shahrazad felt besieged by a culture which validates and propagates everything that is Christian, Western, white, written. With images of Alhambra, when Islamic culture was the bearer of science and art, sliding across the English horizon, she raises her raincoat's collar, and walks on. She had decided to decolonise the mind and the tongue. She had vowed not to utter another word in English. The house of confinement became a ghetto where you shut your ears, eyes, mouth and heart to the host society, like the three wise monkeys.

Her decision was reinforced by the misrepresentation and hostility which reached unprecedented levels during the war. The West was trying to penetrate Baghdad for political and economic reasons. The conflict or quest for oil, territorial expansionism and the multinational corporations' bid for hegemony produced a dominant authority which portrayed the opposition as ignorant and backward. Baghdadis were all tarred with the same black brush, justifying the violence that followed.

The Western media, the so-called fourth authority, paved the way for military action by presenting Baghdadis as either dark, incomprehensible terrorists, or stupid, medieval and rich. They were classified into two groups – one to be fought and "neutralised", the other to be outwitted and conned. Baghdad became "Arabia", an extension of the desert so romantically and faithfully portrayed by Lawrence of Arabia and his predecessors. From a hazy, soft focus painting on the mantelpiece, "Arabia" became part of the West's daily television time.

For the vast majority of Baghdadis the romantic vision of Arabia belonged to the colonial past, together with the books of Burton, Doughty and Lawrence. But for the foreign media, that "Arabia" of the mind still existed and was in constant conflict with the present-day realities of the region. Instead of challenging the handed down misconceptions, most of them were actively consolidating myths of a former age. Western photographers used the camel to reconcile this myth of "Arabia" with the realities of Baghdad at war. Young, closely shaven white soldiers, in sunglasses, were photographed against a backdrop of camels, thus reconciling "Arabia Deserta" with images of an advanced Western world.

Fleet Street obligingly worked on the image of the sultan who until recently had been the bulwark of the West. He began growing horns, exhaling smoke and towering threateningly over "democracy and our way of life". The sultan was inflated until he became so big that his people became him. The Baghdadi people disappeared off the scene – journalistic "collateral damage" of the first kind. You heard the thunder of war, the turkey shoot, but nothing about the defenceless opponents of this mighty war machine. It was a false war which bore a false victory.

Shahrazad was screaming against this latest military adventure, but few people heard. Deafness, which was so eloquently described by John Berger,[9] became endemic. She looked around her, tried to communicate, but got no response apart from polite smiles and small talk. Where does the bird fly after the last sky? Exile became a sentence of solitary confinement.

Shahrazad remembered why she had committed herself to living in exile in the first place. She wanted to safeguard her integrity and the purity of her tales. She wanted to teach her children songs of peace – she would sing loud and clear. She had emigrated in pursuit of democracy and freedom of expression. She left Baghdad when she read Sartre: "One does not write for slaves. The art of fiction is bound up with the only regime in which prose has meaning, democracy."[10] Freedom of expression, and the democracy which she has pursued, were under threat. The moment journalists put on army uniform and began parroting the generals, freedom of expression began receding. Censorship, the corruption of language and the compromise of some journalists, academics and commentators brought back bad memories. That, after all, is why she had left Baghdad. But the dream she had pursued had been shattered. The house of obedience became a house of confinement, then a ghetto, and was slowly becoming a mental hospital.

---

9 John Berger, "In the land of the deaf", the *Guardian*, 2 March 1991.
10 Jean-Paul Sartre, "Why write?", in *20th Century Literary Criticism*, ed. David Lodge (London, Longman, 1972), p. 371.

When you fail to recognise the truth of your experience in the Western perception and representation of it, when you realise that you are – after all these years of living in exile – still dark, incomprehensible, untouchable, and completely surrounded by high white walls, you have very few options left. You become the dark, invisible and ignorant immigrant you are cast as, ever grateful to the host country for allowing you to step on its soil. You begin shrinking in order not to occupy more space than you should. You embrace your inferior position wholeheartedly and bowing becomes part of your life. In short, you become a coconut – white on the inside and black on the out. Hollow on the inside with no spine, substance or colour. Exile becomes the country of coconuts and slavery.

Or you see *Gandhi, Lawrence of Arabia, The Sheltering Sky, Harem, The Jewel in the Crown* and refuse to accept their distorted characters as your representatives. You become so embittered and anguished over seeing yourself mutilated every day on screen that you build a castle around your immigrant heart and refuse to have anything to do with the host society. Like a mole, you live underground, in the darkness. You decide that your native Urdu, Swahili or Arabic is better than their snobbish English. You impose values and ideas on your children long since discarded in your country of origin. Anger and bitterness feed your fundamentalist and puritan ideas. The only self-defence open to you is to shrivel, wrap yourself in black, and hide in the mosque.

But Shahrazad, the oriental storyteller, the immigrant daughter of the vizier, turns her face towards a sky beyond the last sky, and sings with Maya Angelou:

> You may write me down in history
> with your bitter, twisted lies.
> You may trod me in the very dirt
> But still, like dust, I'll rise.[11]

---

11 Maya Angelou, *And Still I Rise* (London, Virago Press, 1986).

Shahrazad, like many other writers in exile, would shake her stick at misrepresentation, reductionism and ignorance. She, the deaf, mute, ignorant native, announces that she has arrived – the character backdrop of a foreign landscape faithfully and romantically described in travel books. "I am here," she says, "the native who never wrote about you behind your back." She tries to imagine herself in Western works – *The Seven Pillars of Wisdom, Cry Freedom, Heart of Darkness*. She watches films made by the host society, like *The Sheltering Sky*, and argues that the vast majority of Baghdadi women have professions other than the oldest one, that Baghdadi men are not lascivious beasts and that the societies of that land have changed since the Western observer first landed. The black experience does not need a white middleman to represent and legitimise it. She begins to talk herself into being, to paint her image into existence, to write herself into their literature.

She realises that Baghdad will be built again by its own people, that palm trees outlast storms, and that brave spirits shall overcome. She unties her sore tongue and begins singing in whatever language comes first. She admires Ngugi, but finds herself standing up and walking out of his puritan camp. She joins the camp of Chinua Achebe where "to throw out the English language in order to restore linguistic justice and self-respect to ourselves is a historical fantasy . . . we needed [the English] language to transact our business, including the business of overthrowing colonialism itself in the fullness of time."[12] The reconciliation with the English language takes place despite her ambiguous feeling towards it. She should celebrate her uniqueness in English, and describe her new world in order to understand it. She should write her colours back into the predominantly white tapestry.

She sings with Achebe "The Song of Ourselves", celebrating differences and similarities, rejecting absolute truths about herself and others, welcoming disruptions of linear narratives, embracing debate, uncertainty and dissent. Standing outside the whale, "in this world

---

12 Chinua Achebe, "The song of ourselves", *New Statesman and Society*, 9 February 1990.

with no safe corners",[13] she sings for bridges, those destroyed and those to be built. The truth is that there is no house apart from the fragile, strong house of writing, the house of song. The song which delivered Shahrazad in the past will deliver her again. She, like many other immigrants and exiles, will survive by building a house of songs. Shahrazad, the immigrant daughter of the vizier, the oriental storyteller, becomes a phoenix, a beautiful, colourful bird of survival, forever flying beyond the last sky.

13 Salman Rushdie, "Outside the whale", *Granta*, 1985.

ALIA MAMDOUH

The writing career of Alia Mamdouh, who was born in 1944 of an Iraqi father and a Syrian mother, has spanned the Arab world in the fields of literature and journalism.

Mamdouh graduated with a degree in psychology in 1971 from the University of Mustansariyya, Iraq. Her first collection of short stories, *Iftitahyya li-l-Dahik* (An Overture for Laughter), was published in Beirut in 1973; this was followed five years later by her second collection of short stories *Hawamish ila al-Sayyida B* (Margins for Mrs B). Her first novel, *Layla wa al-Dhi'b* (Layla and the Wolf), was published in 1981. Her second novel, *Mothballs* (Habat al-Naftalin), was published in English by Garnet Publishing and will be published soon in Italian, Dutch and French. *Al-Wala'* (The Passion), a third novel, was published in 1995.

Mamdouh was also Editor-in-Chief at *al-Rasid* magazine from 1970 to 1982, before taking up a similar position at *al-Fikr al Mu'asir* magazine for two years. Mamdouh continues to contribute to the main newspapers and journals of the Arab world.

She currently lives in Paris.

CREATURES OF ARAB FEAR

ALIA MAMDOUH

The Back Seat

Fear shapes the space of my writing. It has resolved many things and is behind many decisions. No sooner is the cupboard of childhood opened than the aroma of the house – a mixture of fear and submission – wafts into my face and settles there. However, the important thing is that the door is opened even if, on most occasions, its sharp creak grates upon the ear.

I was born, went to school, then to university, graduated, ran away with the one I loved and unloaded the burden of fear onto a man much older than myself who trained me to fear nothing but him. Now I find it difficult to express the true nature of my fear, but it is certainly not only due to male excesses, for page after page of my diaries record the acts of women. They were even more tyrannical and moralistic than the men.

My father was a handsome man, boisterous and good but also tormented by neurosis. He was the first policeman – his profession – I had to face and I was determined to confuse him by being submissive at home and rebellious outside. In addition I used to swing my hips to make up for my ugliness. During those years I became aware of the incongruity that existed between oppressive traditions and the bird who wanted to sing separately from the flock of boys and girls of the family. I was certain that one day I would fly away from them for good. And I withdrew into myself when I understood that they wanted to extract every thought in my head, one by one, like decayed teeth.

You have but one reservoir – your dreams. Let anger and provocation overcome you as you relate your stories and write your novels, while you urge your steps towards the back rows. These rows always used to enchant you and they still do, for here you are left alone. From the back you have a view over everything – the stage, and the ladies and gentlemen of the audience.

I was always late when going to these places, to give me a chance to hide away in the seats at the rear, and I used to tell myself – once at the back, fear shrinks.

Of course, the others were also afraid, but perhaps not in the way that I was. Fear was behind everything I did in my life, everything I made of it. With effective insistence it urged me to write. Injustice and oppression made my blood boil, extracting from me all the pages that I wrote, as if warding off torture.

The women of the family insisted: "be gentle, soft, adorn yourself, fatten up and in the end you will get married and have children." And as night neared its end, you repeated to yourself, "God, grant us victory and let us leave defeat here on the dressing-table. May these assaults on my soul and body inspire my work."

I fought in a metaphorical sense to defend my freedom and independence, and I used an intangible weapon – writing – in order to hold in my hand something different, something tender – my own book.

Woman and Man

It is in my nature never to give up. Extreme fear drives me to the darkest and most dangerous sites. I write about them in "the first person". The critics do not like this type of writing much because it refers to the personal, maybe even to the intimate. And why not? It reshapes the only world allowed to me – that of the self – carrying it forwards with an outstretched hand beyond the boundaries of mere individual self. It is the first, the original person, who stands for all and will say before them: "this is just the beginning". I cannot accept that the object is substituted for the subject. Nor do I bear facile and indifferent chatter easily. As for the craftsmen of the word, the eminent writers, destructive like myself, I spend most of my time in their company. We are in the same tightly sealed bottle.

I have never felt that man is my enemy or rival. He is a man. What does that mean? To some he appears like a tourist on his travels, sometimes preferring monuments to human beings. He is always in a hurry and not always because this is the way of modern life. Usually he sees woman as a mere distraction on his holiday. Thus his picture of her is that of a character in a text or story, perhaps a legend, invisible because he has rejected her reality and turned her into something not altogether credible. And yet, she is able to perform miracles and this she does through the one tool left to her, man himself.

Some people made me laugh at myself and that is a great virtue. My reputation was deteriorating, but I had different standards. Whether I did my work well or not, they would applaud me, calling me their sister. In this respect man came closer to me. He resembled me, and not the other way round.

I grew up and became savage and tormented; I travelled through fiery places, touched the flame, and did not ask for a glove to protect me. We *are* the flame. I do not distinguish between women of my country and women of other countries, for all women are my country. It is not the same for a woman to be ignored, ruined or promoted. I earned all the punishments at birth by being born in the poison of this world. But let us ask with joy, how does this deficient woman give birth to a flawless boy?

Members of the Family

I never joined any party. I never fought with any team. My goal to become a true writer allowed me no concessions.

Night awaited you like the most faithful companion and the midday heat was your garden. You used to struggle behind closed doors while on the left bank of the river you could see the image of your country's parties, Marxist and nationalist, respected by all. Yet this image was comprised of men who, in general, were the bureaucratic civil servants with whom the parties were packed. The parties were thus either turned into graves or to dens of corruption instead of being places leading men to freedom and independence. If this is the fate of aspiring men, what then of women?

In my family there were no leaders or fighters, not even any politicians. The men in my family were ordinary men, those you meet in small streets and narrow alleyways. They were lowly civil servants whose lives were divided between insomnia and illness. They did not go to jail and did not inherit any sense of class struggle. They were so ordinary it was almost as though they were in disguise. If someone told them of his misfortune, they would simply turn the other way, pray for protection from the Devil and repeat: "May God be with us, not against us." My family's behaviour in public derived from the secret fear which lived in everyone, rotating in an ever widening circle, from the living room to the shared bedrooms, encompassing the school, the street, and even public baths. Fear haunted every member of this family. They used to call it humanity and friendliness, refer to it as kinship and pride. I still have not learnt its true name. Let us hope that writing will reveal it. It is embedded in all that happened in those years, in the white pages which await the suitcase to be opened so that they can be clothed. I look at the members of this family as if we were not yet out of the tunnel. But were I to touch them, to feel their warmth, then I would be shouted at: "Look, she still behaves as though she were at primary school!"

Creatures of Fear

So, it is fear alone. It has been with me all my life. The older I get, the more I control the factors that give rise to it. One day it felt as if it had replaced the very blood in my veins, so intimate was it. It runs through families, clans and perhaps even in nations. It is the source of pleasure, pain and the highest state of oblivion. It is the body's bitter taste, whether attractive or repellent. It resides in our walls and our foundations, in our vaults and our domes, between our keys and our locks, forever sheltered in the structure of language and the poverty of human relations. It is in every drawer; no head is free of it and its stamp is on every literary text. Thus our Arab fear appears to be a multi-headed monster feeding on the poison which stems from our conditioning to submit, to fragment and to keep it all to ourselves. It is our upbringing which, upon analysis, proves utterly dangerous, even criminal. In the end it is what justifies a cycle of personal writing inspired by our tormented and artificial lives in the Arab World.

Fear is something invisible, manifest only through its consequences. Like a soldier, the writer must carry out patrols in the battleground to survey dangerous places. And when we are certain we have left the first home, fear, then the road will carry us upwards to a crossroads both wonderful and terrifying – freedom. There you stand alone and free. And is this not the one fruit worthy to nourish your very core? Is it not your raw material? Waste no time, this is the site you want to excavate and from now on not a single line will resonate of anything else. Go on excavating with both bitterness and compassion even if it does not yet mean anything. But here you are, doing a job which *will* bring your brethren back to reality and open up their hearts while you are growing ever closer to the self you are longing to find.

Writing and Questions

In this section I shall raise some questions which may appear to be contradictory. When appearing in newspapers, reviews or magazines, they are dealt with superficially as if they were only of marginal interest, like fleeting pastimes. Creative writing is treated with an insubstantial aura of charitable intention as if it were some sort of trendy social must.

1   Can publishers and distributors make a profit out of Arab women's writing?
2   Is there a (contemporary) Arab woman writer whose work fills the shelves, who is well distributed, influential and who earns her living through writing?
3   Why do our books sell so poorly?
4   Is female creativity still perceived as undesirable? Could this be the reason women's works rarely reach either the élite or the wider public?
5   Why do some women writers not believe in their abilities and lack self-confidence? Why are they not more arrogant?
6   Has the Arab woman writer reached the ultimate point of spiritual evolution? And what are the obstacles she has faced in this decade? Have they changed in the last quarter of a century?
7   This is a very sensitive question, but one the public wants an answer to: what is the extent of autobiography in the woman writer's work?
8   Is it really true, as has been contended, that women first, do not have creative ability, and second, cannot bear the isolation that creativity, by its very nature, surreptitiously imposes upon them?
9   Does the Arab woman artist ever ask herself this difficult question: what would happen to her if for some reason she was no longer able to write?
10 Does the woman writer only write for fame? Is her true aim to become a star? How does she put up with fame since it also has a frightening side and intrudes upon the isolation so vital to creative writing?
11 Why are women writers so sensitive to criticism? Is it because, unconsciously, criticism tells them once more that they are "only women" and therefore criticism should deal with them more gently than with male writers?

Finally, I feel that I circulate freely between male and female writers. We are examining the building together, with the same tools, repeating amongst ourselves that we must try and try again without complacency or arrogance.

To conclude, we must be brave and accept that which turned our fear into a friend, and turned simplicity into creativity. Let us stand at the threshold of writing, which is also the threshold of all possibilities, allowing us to gain access to both the reader and that secret self who perhaps still crouches in the back row . . .

SAMIRA AL-MANA'

Samira al-Mana' was born in Basra, Iraq, in 1935, but has lived in self-imposed exile in Britain for the past twenty-five years. Al-Mana' was educated in Iraq, at the University of Baghdad, where she studied for a BA Honours degree in Arabic Language. She then went on to teach Arabic language and literature in a secondary school in Baghdad. Once in Britain, she undertook a Postgraduate Diploma in Librarianship and worked between 1976 and 1980 as Chief Librarian at the Iraqi Cultural Centre in London.

Al-Sabiqun wa-l-Lahiqun (The Forerunners and the Newcomers) was al-Mana''s first novel and was published in Beirut in 1972. Her second novel, *Al-Thuna'iyya al-Lundaniyya* (A London Sequel) was published almost six years later. In the intervening period, al-Mana' produced *Al-Ghina'* (Singing) – a collection of short stories, in 1976. Her play, *Only a Half*, was published in 1984. Her third novel, *Habl al-Surra* (The Umbilical Cord) was published in 1990. Al-Mana' is currently Assistant Editor at the *al-Ightirab al-Adabi*, a magazine which deals specifically with the literature of exile. The magazine has serialised her latest novel, *Shufuni Shufuni* (Look At Me, Look At Me).

WRITING AND THE NOTION OF SEARCHING
FOR FEMALE IDENTITY

SAMIRA AL-MANA'

To start with, there are high walls and no windows. The openings in the rooms face inwards, only inwards. The region is remote, the desert arid, the people conservative. The girls there wear black cloaks. This one is aged between eleven and twelve. What is there to amuse a lonely little girl alone among adults in the desolate Zubair region? Games, parks, friends – none of these exist. All she has are rags from which she creates the faces and bodies of her dolls. These she treats as human for she needs them as family and friends. This one is the sister, this the daughter, this the stern father of whom all are afraid. Sometimes she goes with her family to Basra town, twenty minutes by car from Zubair. All at once, endless greenery stretches before her eyes. Rivers, markets, cafés, unveiled women, vitality in abundance. She accepts the contradiction between the two regions as the norm, part of the nature of things. She returns to their silent home in the arid region, compliant and forbearing, as if facing the inevitable.

Henceforth contradiction intrigues her, becoming a source of amusement, surprise and adventure. And what of the possibility of discovering books in this mute and dreary house – controversial, congenial, serious, sad, exhilarating books, bringing her a world full of its own contradictions? So her desire to seek and become familiar with that world waxes stronger, whilst the members of her family take their siesta in the heat of the Iraqi summer or busy themselves with their everyday affairs. The books covering some of the walls of the house belong to her father or her elder brother; they include old ones with yellowed pages which are precious to the former, such as *al-'Iqd al-Farid* (The Unique Necklace), and shiny new ones which are the passion of the latter. There are books which tell of the distant past, of the latest developments in the Second World War, and of what man has done to his fellow man; there are books, too, of romance and desire, of rose-tinted letters and love-nests, of the man whom all strive to keep her from touching and whom they prevent from making contact with the hems of her clothes.

When she reaches the age of twelve, others' awareness of her grows. They wrap her in a cloak as if she were prey. Doors must be locked around her. Any objection? Why? She lets them practise the arts of fear on her in numerous forms. She looks at them and says nothing. She is a spectator; to her they are phantoms compared to her real companions in the folds of pages. One person marrying another is of no consequence to her. What's all the fuss about? But when the magician advises Zanuba, heroine of the novel *'Awdat al-Ruh* (The Return of the Soul) by Egyptian author Tawfiq al-Hakim, to use the hoopoe bird for a marriage prescription, this for her is reality.

As if someone is watching over her with care and compassion, within a short time she sees her society shake off its black cloak and begin to evolve slowly but surely without forced intervention. It is as though the Iraqi woman allowed to go to school a generation earlier had persuaded it to open the windows a little and let clean air enter the musty places. The magical prescription of education soon enables the girl to get up off her knees without making demands, taking part in noisy demonstrations or declaring war. In education she finds the splendid remedy which saved her grandmother Shahrazad from the claws of the villainous Shahrayar. She swiftly casts off the cloak without attracting much attention in the streets of Iraq's biggest towns. She is accepted in a co-educational college in Baghdad University, as if the restrictions she was forced to endure during her early years in Zubair were a laughable, trifling matter.

Finally, in the second year of teacher training college at Baghdad University, she finds the words to express her situation, to release what has been imprisoned in her chest for all these years. The opportunity suddenly presents itself when she sits her mid-year composition examination. She chooses the moment to write a few lines about a flower:

> "I was blind, alone and speechless." Thus the lemon flower spoke to me as I was about to pluck it and bind it with its dewy sister flowers into a necklace to adorn my neck this evening. I was completely taken aback by her fervent pleas to be left alone for one day, the day of her birth and emergence into the light.
>
> Slowly, I lifted my hand from her branch, entranced by its perfume. I yearned to stand beside her and inhale her amazing scent.
>
> She smiled a radiant smile adorned with sparkling dewdrops, and said: "The world! I know everything about the world, love and goodness, hatred and meanness, hope and disappointment. Yes, I know it all. I did not discover it today, I did not learn it when my petals opened and my fragrance issued forth. No indeed, I have known it since the old days, long old days within the walls of my thick wrapping, days which I spent eavesdropping and fidgeting, listening to my sister flowers on moonlit nights as they chatted and exchanged their delicious small talk. How they laughed and joked! God knows how I longed to join them and join in their conversations. But now you want to pluck me. Today I am newly born, so how can I die?"

Her kindly teacher takes the paper from her. He is full of praise and enthusiasm for it, and eager to publish it in the Ministry's official magazine. And indeed it is published. Those few lines are a distillation of all that has gone on in her mind for years, and one way or another

will continually find an echo in her novels and short stories over the
coming years.

She is a woman searching for compassion, understanding and
justice in a man's world raging with cruelty, oppression and indifference. Here she finds herself outside the society of forbearing women,
silent women, wailing women devoid of strength and power; at odds
with the Iraqi singer on the radio who intoxicates her audience when
she croons "My husband took a young girl to wife", or entertains them
and makes them laugh with,

> All night long he beats me with bamboo,
> Go ask the neighbours, what did I do?

I look around me and begin to worry, wonderful enriching worry.
I begin to dare, and suddenly feel deprived. I was content with what
was conferred on me before, satisfied with the books I read. Most of
the authors were men, and I used to read them with eagerness and
pride. Now, all at once I feel sad, unable to be happy unless I write
what I want to say. I am dissatisfied with other people's writing.
Others remain others. I do not want to pick up the crumbs from
their table. I want to give my own opinion, to be myself, to be true to
my experience, to what concerns me, to what is important to me, to
make such and such a matter my priority and leave other things till
last. My priorities are not theirs. Woman's evil is not the same as
man's, otherwise why would wars take place and why would her
young children take up arms? It is not woman who snuffs out life and
violates the birth of a flower. To paraphrase the words of a leading
woman writer, Anaïs Nin:

> When I was young, I was afraid to become a writer and was not one
> until the age of twenty, twenty-one or twenty-two. I depended on
> those writers I knew, hoping that they would write for me what
> I wanted to say. I let them revolt on my behalf, write for me.
> Suddenly I realised that I was wrong to expect this of them. I
> believe that men will be relieved of this burden which is imposed on
> them by the other side. It is my own task to be a voice for women.

AHLEM MOSTEGHANEMI

Ahlem Mosteghanemi's first collection of poetry, *'Ala Marf' al-Ayyam*, was published in 1973, the same year that she received her degree in literature from the University of Algeria. Mosteghanemi belongs to what came to be known as the first 'arabised' generation of university graduates in Algeria after independence.

Mosteghanemi's novel *Al-Kitaba fi Lahzati 'Uri* (Writing at the Moment of Nakedness) was published in 1976. In 1980 she undertook her P.h.D. in Sociology at the Sorbonne. Her supervisor, the renowned sociologist Jacques Berque wrote the introduction to Mosteghanemi's 1982 publication, *Algérie, Femmes et Ecritures*, a study of women writers in Algeria.

Mosteghanemi's novel *Dhakirat al-Jasad* (The Body's Memory) was published in 1993. This was the first novel to be written in Arabic by a woman writer in Algeria. Mosteghanemi commented: "This fact fills me with horror, not pride. How could I be the first poetess in Arabic, and twenty years later the first woman novelist writing in Arabic in a country where thousands of women graduate and master the Arabic language."

Writing against time
and history

Ahlem Mosteghanemi

One day, someone comes and asks you to talk about your experience of writing. Then you, who made writing your profession, do not know how to summarise your life on paper, nor say exactly when you were born. For a writer is born suddenly but generally not on the date expected. There are those who believe that they were always destined to be a writer, those who were born as writers before their first book was published and some who were not born until their forties in the presence of their latest text. If dozens of pages are drafted, this does not make you a creative artist, and even if more than one book is published, this does not make you a writer. Hemingway used to say: "A writer is someone who has readers." Perhaps he meant someone who has admirers and enemies.

To write means to think against yourself, to argue, to oppose, to take a risk, to be aware from the start that there is no literature other than the prohibited, no creativity outside the forbidden, and only large questions to which there are no answers. And if writing were not a continual examination of the "acceptable", humanity would be content with religious books and matters would end there; but the risks and pleasures of writing lie in its being a review and continual questioning of the self, in other words, an everlasting adventure.

Thus I am able to say that the poet in me was born at the age of eighteen, in a hall crammed full of men. It was a poetry evening and I stood up to read a romantic poem to a wild and ardent Algerian audience. Half had come to applaud me, the other half to condemn my femininity and my writing about love at a time when martyrs were still being buried on the pages of newspapers and between the covers of books. What added to the ardour of the hall was my reputation in the media as the presenter of a programme of romantic poetry, broadcast every evening under the title *Whispers*.

In essence, this programme was a challenge to the Algerian national character, which was neither used to hearing nor to reciting love poetry. So how could it come from an Algerian girl who was one of the blossoms of the generation of independence which was totally dedicated to the cause of revolution?

In reality, we were a people suffering from lack of romance for complex historical reasons. I do not know how I discovered this, despite my youth. I made love and the beautiful word my primary cause, believing that the Algerian character was sick and void within, that all the edifice and the revolutionary slogans erected around it after independence would not help to construct it. Only language and emotions are capable of restoring and rebuilding a new Algeria. Perhaps one of the causes of our present problems is our neglect, after the revolution, of the emotional and psychological make-up of people and our preoccupation with agriculture and an exemplary economy.

That day, those hostile male voices would have drowned out my embarrassed and poetic recitation and suffocated my voice which was coming out for the first time, but I found my strength in a man whom I feared and of whom I was perhaps shy.

I had planned that the poetry evening would coincide with my father being in hospital to ensure that he could not be present and hear what I was writing. I knew that he could not read me because he did not know Arabic. In fact, my strength and courage to write lay in the ignorance of all the members of my family of Arabic, including my father, who was a poet writing in French, who never asked me what I was writing although he looked at my photos in the newspapers with paternal pride.

But my father, who was in a military hospital for treatment, found out about this evening from the newspapers and promptly decided to leave hospital without permission from the doctor, having paid his nurses a sum of money to escort him.

I recall nearly fainting when, from my platform, I saw my father, surrounded by nurses, enter the hall and take his seat before me.

I had not expected, when I had chosen deliberately provocative poems, that my father would be listening to me. Reluctantly, I continued reading since I had no other poems with me. My final surprise came at the end of the evening when some of the audience began attacking me for omitting the Algerian revolution from my poetry. Then my father stood up and asked to speak in his capacity as my father. I remember him saying: "My daughter was born during the revolution and she can neither write about something that she has not lived nor fabricate memories so as to be a poet in your eyes. She is not here to write history but to write her feelings. Do not kill poetry, too, in the name of the revolution. If you want to talk about the revolution, it is I who will talk about it with you since I am a *mujahid* [holy warrior] whereas she is from another generation which today has other concerns."

To my astonishment, an argument began between my father and the hall. Half the hall began to applaud him as he responded on my behalf in refined language and with conviction. The other half of the participants, who did not understand the desperate struggle of this father in defence of his daughter and of the glory of poetry rather than the glory of the revolution or of the tribe, were taken by surprise.

Nobody noticed his tears as he kissed me at the close of the evening and left the hall with his nurses to return to his hospital room. I wept when I saw him retreat with the pride and leave me to return home alone, as if showing me that on that day a path had appeared which

I would walk alone, that he would not always be there to defend me. I felt a combination of bitterness and pride. My father had broken hospital rules and had come for two hours to save me, despite myself, from my first flaying. I was not aware that day, being eighteen years old, that I had lost a city and gained a father and that afterwards nobody would be able to defeat me or insult me; but I did know that in order to confront a male-dominated society I would have to ensure the presence of a man by my side.

In connection with this incident, I now remember with pain that this poetry evening of mine was part of the 1973 poetry festival in which youth poetry in two languages, French and Arabic, was given the largest coverage. My evening of poetry was between the recitals of al-Taher Ja'ut and Yusif Sabti, who used to write in French and whose poetic journey began with me at the same festival. We did not know then that, despite the quiet and the indifference with which the audience greeted them, and the storm of publicity that I received and for which they envied me, a day would come twenty years later when they alone would hit the headlines in all the foreign and Arabic newspapers. But they would make the news not as poets but as martyrs to Algerian poetry, butchered on our behalf, shot dead, charged simply with writing.[1]

That was a time of beautiful challenge. Even though I was the only girl to write amongst the poets writing in Arabic and French, I have always felt that my identification with the dreams and enthusiasm of that generation of young people exceeded my feminine identity, that poetry and country are my primary cause. As for being a woman, that is my problem alone.

This was confirmed to me a number of years later when I left Algeria to settle in France and entered the whirlpool of married life, motherhood and social obligations.

One morning I awoke to find myself a wife, mother of three children, holder of a doctorate from the Sorbonne, researcher in

---

1 Since the cancellation of the election in Algeria in 1992 and the beginning of the civil unrest, about sixty journalists and writers have been killed.

sociology, cook, washerwoman, cleaner and nursemaid at all hours of the day. I had numerous roles and jobs, but I had lost the title of poet. I do not say that I had given up poetry, but rather that it had left me and given me up because I had grown inferior to it.

For to be a poet means to be a completely free human being. I do not only mean to be free to express your opinion or to be free to go crazily saying or doing what you want; I also mean being free with your time. To be a poet means behaving like a poet, as if you have consecrated yourself to it. For, like all creativity, it comes to you whenever it wants, upsets your plans when it wants, cancels your appointment for you, imposes another on you, holds you for hours in front of paper, takes you out of your daily round – luxuries not within the scope of a woman in our country. If a poet is married, he is of necessity half a poet. So what then if the poet is an Arab woman with a number of children and a number of social jobs and surrounded by more than one official and family censor – she is simply a "bit-part poet".

If I discovered that poetry had deserted me, it did not scare me as much as the frightening thought that writing would leave me too. Words obsess me, for I am a woman of paper and am used to living between the covers of books. I love and hate and rejoice and mourn and commit every transgression on paper. I have learned to be a creature of words and not to shrink from seeing myself naked and trembling on paper, for I love my nakedness, love the tremor of my naked body before the pool of ink. I believe it is only those words which strip us bare that resemble us, whereas those that clothe us deform us. This is why the title of my second book in twenty years is *al-Kitaba fi Lahzati 'Uri* (Writing at the Moment of Nakedness).

Perhaps the life of motherhood and home which I have lived for fifteen consecutive years has effected a change in my mood and in my view of writing because it is no longer my whole life. I have grown more attractive and more dangerous. I have developed "ink sickness" and suffer fear and terror of something impossible to define. I have become fragmented and capable of living inside more than one woman, with more than one weather forecast a day, more than one body a night, more than one heart and more than one mood of passion. But had I only one hand and no more, I would write all this with it. And steal all this with it.

Jean Genet said, "Before, I used to steal. Today, I write books." I say the opposite: I started out a writer and ended up a thief. If, for some people, writing is a luxury and a status symbol, for me it is confrontation with reality. It is continual robbery and break-in, for I steal time to write, break into my son's study to write and cheat on those around me to make a date with paper. I continue stealing words like some people steal happiness, because writing is the only adventure worth the risk and I have to live it with the danger of loss, like a pleasure under threat.

I spent many years without a study, without a room for books, carrying my papers from room to room, sometimes writing on the kitchen table, sometimes in the dining-room or on my bed in the bedroom. Now I wonder whether it was because all the rooms around me were reserved that I grew used to living inside myself and because all the doors around me were closed that one day I accidently opened a door which had to be opened and suddenly there I was before myself, a novelist.

Louis Aragon has a beautiful saying: "The novel is the key to forbidden rooms in our house." The day I read it I realised that my real birth was the day I opened that door to see a woman whom I had expected to be someone else. Suddenly, I was overcome by dizziness and astonishment and a torrent of words swept me towards an open text, frightening in its effusion. I would produce nothing less than a novel whose length would be four hundred pages, entitled *Dhakirat al-Jasad* (The Body's Memory).

I discovered that I had spent my life bypassing those forbidden rooms within me, believing that they did not concern me since I lived somewhere else. In reality, I did live in other rooms and it was they that inhabited me and occupied the largest domain of my inner space and my space on paper. Thus their keys controlled me and their locks were the holes to my freedom and my servitude.

I realised that in order to be a writer I had to live in a glasshouse and not hide behind books of fortified cement, for the novelist does not hesitate to open secret doors before you; the novelist dares to invite you to visit the lower floors of the house and the cellars and locked places in which dust and old furniture and memories gather, and every corridor of the self where electricity is not yet installed and from where a suspicious stale smell emanates.

It is he who opens the door for you in ordinary clothes, or in his underwear, without being concerned that he has forgotten to wash his face and shave and take off his nightshirt to welcome you. His excuse for this is that his life resembles your own, his particulars do not differ from yours, and you bought his book to read about none other than yourself.

But in spite of this, I must admit that whatever our integrity, we also write to deceive.

Those who claim that they write to be as honest as possible make me laugh in their naïvety or in their outright dishonesty. For writing is a continual evasion of the self, an endless deception of others, a test of their power to read blank white pages and the power of time to preserve the blackness of the words.

In fact, we always write our text outside the text and thus in all our books there is a completely blank page which is our real story. This page is the coffin of the words which will die with us, for the coffin of a writer, like his life, is nothing but what remains of the blanks in his book and what remains of the blank pages on this table.

For eternity we have been writing knowing full well that in the final analysis every book awaits a checkpoint searching our thoughts, interpreting our dreams, lying in wait for us between sentences, explaining our silences and the gaps between our words.

What is new is that we used to write for an anonymous reader whereas now we write for an anonymous killer who condemns us according to his mood. We used to know the censor and either confront him or outwit him, but now we do not know who controls whom or what the new yardsticks for writing are.

What is new in writing today is that the suppression used to come from the authorities and from the family whereas now it comes from the reader himself. Whereas we used to dream of writing new books, in Algeria we dream of republishing our old ones and what we used to write in the 1970s we cannot write today.

Whereas we used to dream of living one day with what we write, we now dream of not dying one day because of what we write.

Whereas we used to write dreaming of a country to die for, we now write for a country at whose hands we are dying.

In the beginning we used to dream of emigrating and becoming famous writers abroad. Today we have become this way. Today we dream of returning home for a few days and of living there incognito.

Twenty years ago I dreamed of one day receiving an invitation from Paris to deliver a lecture there. Today I hope to receive an invitation from Algeria to give that same lecture there and to return safely to my children.

Twenty years ago I dreamed of reading poetry in Beirut to an educated public but two years ago, when I read a poem in Beirut, I left the hall crying. After all these years, I discovered that my real hope was to read poetry only in Algeria and that I would not be a poet except in my own country.

In the end, I have grown accustomed to the rituals of the bullfight and that malicious crowd who come to bait my blood and go home carrying my ear in their pocket as does the matador with the defeated bull.

Yes, our dreams have been greatly humbled in a short time. The national defeats and disappointments have exhausted us. Between a time of death and a time of stupor, we have entered a time of opposition to writing.

If this reality is a writer's Hell and death, its advantage is to restore the value of writing and a chance to reconsider for those who have long cheapened the word and insulted the honour of the pen.

They should realise that there is no longer a text without a cost and that the time has come for those who are not writers to withdraw and leave this Hell to others who are splendid writers and who are living martyrs of the word, like my friend, the writer Zaynab al-'Aaraj and her novelist husband, Wasini al-'Aaraj, and Rashid Bujadra and Rashid Mimuni. Dozens of dispersed Algerian artists searching for shelter for themselves and their children and for a small patch a little larger than a tomb, and a little smaller than a homeland, in which to live and write. To them I present this testimony of mine which is inferior to the testimony of their present lives and possibly of their future death. As for what I have said to you today, in reality it is not worth remembering and does not equal one drop of the blood of al-Taher Ja'ut nor Yusif Sabti or any of the martyrs to Algerian writing.

HAMIDA NAʿNA

Born and educated in Syria, Hamida Naʿna began her literary career in 1971, the same year she graduated from Damascus University. *Anashid li Imraʾa la Taʿrif al-Farah* (Anthems for a Woman Who Does Not Know Happiness) was Naʿnaʾs first book of poems.

A postgraduate degree in literature and Islamic studies from the Sorbonne was followed by three years of work for UNESCO. Naʿnaʾs subsequent work as a journalist as head of the European and North African bureau at *as-Safir* newspaper led to her interviewing a number of prominent thinkers and writers. These interviews with Michel Foucault, Roland Barthes, Jean-Paul Sartre, Simone de Beauvoir, Nathalie Sarraute, Aimé Césaire, Octavio Paz and Leopold Senghor were published in 1990 in a book entitled *Hiwarat maʿ Mufakiri al-Gharb* (Debates with Western Thinkers). This book followed the publication of another work of non-fiction, *al-Subh al-Dami fi ʾAdan* (The Bloody Morning in Eden) in 1987 which investigated the split of the Yemeni Socialist party. Two of her novels, *The Homeland* (Al-Watan fi-l-ʿAynayn) and *Man Yajruwʾ ʿala al-Shawq* (Who Dares To Yearn?), were published in 1989; the latter was also translated into German. Her political and literary memoirs, *Min*

Dafater Imra'a (From the Notebooks of a Woman), were published in 1992. Na'na currently lives in Paris with her French husband. She is a senior correspondent for the French magazine *Le Nouvel Afrique-Asie* and also contributes regularly to several Arabic newspapers.

WRITING AWAY THE PRISON

HAMIDA NA'NA

❧◗◉◖☙

Was it just an accident that my mother sent me to school to learn to
read and write? Perhaps not, since she wanted to rid the house of her
naughty and obstinate daughter and imitate my feudal uncle's family.
They had sent their daughter, who was my age, to school. So there I
was, the first child in a family of nine, going to school to learn to
read and write. Today I cannot recall that distant past in detail, but
I do know that my first day at school took on a funereal character
at home. The family regarded it as sinful, and the neighbourhood
ridiculed it. How could a mother think of teaching her daughter to
read and write? Wasn't she afraid she would write to her lovers when
she grew up? Perhaps I justified this fear when I became a writer
– for wasn't this shame itself? Then there were the neighbourhood
sheikhs; from where did they get the ready-made *fatwa* (religious
edict) which stated that "Educating girls is *haram* (forbidden)"?
In later years, I plunged into the *Hadith* (sayings) of the Prophet and
the Qur'an trying to find the source of this quotation but was never

able to find a religious text to support it. Myths are found throughout illiterate and poor societies which commonly subject any innovation to religious scrutiny and forbid it. These myths remain widespread and are the secret behind what is called "religious fundamentalism". As for me, I was simply a daughter of a poor, ignorant and wretched society remote from the modern world. In 1946 my country of origin, Syria, had only been independent for eleven years; the houses in Idlib, where I came from in the north of the country had no electricity. The town was a mixture of nationalities – there were remnants of Turks, Kurds, Armenians and Arabs – which were so intermingled that the boundaries between them had disappeared and they had all merged into one Arab culture. Although my father came from an old established family, our home was not rich since he had lost his money gambling and always avoided family burdens and responsibility. When I was young, I realised I was poor, though there was nothing shameful in that. I realised I was a woman, which meant I was of a lower status than my brothers, whom custom dictated I had to serve and whose wishes I had to carry out, however hard and difficult. When I was young, I realised that my primary concern had to be the man, which meant marriage and children. When I was young, I realised I was a shameful being which ate and slept and lived. When I was young, I came to understand the harsh traditions which forbade me as a girl to listen to any discussion which referred to men, marriage or sex. My brother would shoo me away from any gathering in which women gossiped about relations with their husbands.

At school I came to see another world. I learned to read and write. I adored books, the paper they were written on, the script. The only books I had ever seen at home were the Qur'an and the legends of Abi Zaid al-Hilali and Jalila wa Kulaib. I can remember a man with a beautiful voice reading aloud, by lantern light, the story of "The Wanderings of the Bani Halal Tribe", and how they migrated from the Najd to Tunisia. The tribe was only able to enter Tunis because Sa'da was a traitor. Sa'da was the daughter of Zanati Khalifa, the governor of the city, and had fallen in love with a member of the tribe. She opened the gates of the city to them and thereby betrayed her family . . . At this point in the story, those listening heaped curses on Sa'da's head. Then, when they became aware of me silently listening, they reprimanded me and told me to go to bed so that I would not retain anything that I had heard. But I would sleep and dream of Tunis and the tribe's journey and the young man with whom Sa'da had fallen in love . . . My story began in the same way.

When I began my fourth year at school, my family was no longer able to buy books and clothes since frost had ruined the olive crop which was the mainstay of the town. My mother went to the headmistress and told her of our difficulties. The headmistress, who was unmarried, decided to adopt this clever girl and support her. She took me to her home and gave me a room, where I had electricity for the first time in my life. I had previously done my homework by lamplight in a corner of the house. But after a week I ran back to my family. I consider that my first foolhardy experience away from my family, my first risk in returning to them. It was an incident which influenced my whole life.

When I finished primary school, they forced me to wear the *hijab* (veil). I was thirteen years old and considered a woman, so my family had to find a husband for me lest I bring shame upon them. "The angels will kill a pig for every day that passes after a girl becomes a woman and remains single" was the saying that the ignorant *sheikhs* repeated to my father, and he believed it.

I started fighting with my brothers when they tried to prevent me continuing my education. More than once they seized my books and burned them in front of me while I cried and begged them to stop. They were prepared to use all possible means to prevent me from going to school.

When I was fourteen years old, my older brother found a letter a boy of my age had written to me. It created a storm. They held me prisoner in a dark room for more than fifteen days with only dry bread to eat plus any leftovers that my sister, who was two years older than me and who had never been to school, could smuggle in to me.

They burned all my books, even my pencils and notebooks, and prevented me from leaving the room. From then onwards, the whole world came to resemble a big prison. Despite having travelled across four continents, I still carry the prison inside me. Even in the middle of the wide Alianos plain in Colombia I felt imprisoned and wept. My French husband did not understand why I should cry while looking at one of the most vast plains in the world.

Was it a miracle which brought Sheikh Jalil, my father's cousin, on a visit from Ma'arat al-Nu'man? Perhaps it was. He told my family they were making a mistake and prevented my brothers, who were taking turns guarding the room where I was held, from killing me. He persuaded them to release me and also told me to repent. I did not know why or for what I should repent. My brother took out a knife, which was big enough to slaughter a cow, and said to me, "This is for looking at men."

After a huge battle following my rejection of a proposal of marriage from a man twenty-five years older than me, and after convincing my mother that when my education was complete I would help her bring up the rest of my brothers, I was allowed to continue at school until I obtained my *baccalauréat*.

I had to wash my brothers' clothes, clean the house, fetch water from the well, obey the orders of everyone at home as if I were a servant, just so that I could continue my education. I read by moonlight, by lamplight, when everybody was sleeping. I burned my bedclothes more than once and was punished by not being allowed to go to school for several days.

School meant freedom. I used to dream of the day when I would complete my education and be independent, when I would prove to my family that I was capable of earning my living and, above all, that I was honourable and did not look at men.

And so I feared all men. But an intelligent woman teacher made me enrol in a political party while I was still at secondary school. This party was to change the course of my life. For the first time, I realised that I had another family which was more progressive than my biological family. This family was the Party. For the first time, I realised that it was possible to fight to change conditions in a wretched society like mine. For the first time, I had my own secrets which I kept hidden from my family. To put it simply I became, as my comrades would say, "a political activist".

During this period, I read a great deal. I concentrated primarily on nineteenth-century Russian novels. I dreamed of Tolstoy; I cried with Gorky's mother; I experienced the Russian forest with Gogol, and heard the roar of the Draina river. Once, during an oral exam, my geography teacher spread out a map of the world before me. She told me to place one foot of the pair of compasses on my city, Idlib, and then open the instrument out as far as it would go and find the end of the world. The map was circular and the furthest point the compasses could reach was Colombia, which I believed to be the end of the world. I did not know that the Pacific Ocean lay beyond, and Japan further still. I dreamed of going to the end of the world one day and I wanted God to grant my mother's supplications; whenever I behaved badly she called on Him to banish me to Fes and Meknès (my mother believed Fes lay at the end of the world). I laughed when I visited Fes for a conference on creative writing. My mother, bless her, did not know that the Atlantic Ocean lay beyond Fes and then Colombia and the Pacific and that, one day, I would actually reach the end of the world.

The good marks I achieved in my *baccalauréat* earned me a scholarship to a Syrian university. However, when the subject of my going to Damascus University was raised at home, there was an outcry. The illiterate *sheikhs* worked hard to find *fatwas* proving that it was forbidden for girls to mix with boys or travel a long way from their family or think of continuing their studies beyond a certain level.

I do not know how many tears I shed on those cold nights as I begged God, in whom I believed, to put an end to my ordeal and persuade them to allow me to go to university. Half the young men of the family volunteered to marry me to prevent the shame I would bring upon them by enrolling at university. Everything was shameful and forbidden. I began to see the whole world as shameful and forbidden.

Once again my rebellious streak saved me and after I had threatened to commit suicide or to run away, my family agreed that I could go, on the condition that I wore the veil and promised never to speak to my male colleagues. Bound by these harsh conditions, and after the city's mayor had intervened personally since he considered it a waste that such a brilliant student should not continue her education, I enrolled in the Arabic Language Department at Damascus University. I went to live on the university campus and, for the very first time in my life, I had a room of my own and a certain amount of freedom.

In Damascus, I became acquainted with the worlds of my fellow students who came from different cities and countries. I discovered political commitment; I discovered culture, but I remained terrified of approaching men. Throughout the years, my brothers frequently visited me to reassure themselves that their honour was intact. Each time they left me with a host of threats, saying that they would kill me if ever they heard a shameful word about me, and uttering enough warnings to last for several years.

After a year at university, I discovered love and freedom at the same time and decided to rebel against my family. I took off the veil. In my second year I started working as a journalist and my name began appearing in newspapers and on the radio. Then I decided to take part in a television programme with a number of men – it turned out to be a disaster.

This time I really believed they were going to kill me. They all came, all the men of the family, and the decision was taken to finish me off. I can still remember the threats they made and the curses and epithets they used. But once again, the Party intervened to save me, not from the class enemies I had learned about, but from my own people and family.

Then came the defeat of 1967.

I did not see it as a political defeat, but rather as a defeat of the principles I had learned, the promises that the Party had made, and the freedom I had been looking for. I rebelled violently. I left university, Syria and the Party, and joined the armed resistance in Jordan. I felt I would rather die than believe that everything I had been promised was a lie and everything I had done in the cause of freedom had simply been a fistful of wind.

The resistance movement in Amman was made up of people of a mixture of ideologies and thoughts. Amman was the first city in which I felt responsible for my own life and death. But the men and society there judged me even more harshly than my family had, for how could a girl leave her family to live among men, even for the sake of her country?

Sadness was not far off. I lost the man I loved who had introduced me to the Resistance; he was killed in front of me in heavy fighting in one of the villages in the occupied Golan Heights. I had to drag his body to safety under a hail of bullets which rained down around me from the Israeli soldiers. I was twenty years old at the time, and he was two years older. I looked at him laid out in front of me on the red soil. I looked at his face and decided not to cry, so that the others would not see my tears.

In the meantime, my family searched for a lost daughter; society and the Party considered me an outlaw, and the political leadership regarded me as a troublemaker whom it was impossible to control. After my experience in Amman with the resistance movement and with death, I became more pliant and yielded to society's conventions. I returned to my studies and graduated with a degree in literature from the Arabic Language Department.

Once again, chance radically changed my life. I met my first husband, the Minister of Education. Following the resignation of the government to which he belonged, he transferred to the media and became director of a group of government newspapers. I was then press officer at the Ministry of Information. My husband knew all about my past, for the story of my courage in carrying my friend's body under a hail of bullets had gone round political circles.

With the military coup which brought Hafez al-Assad to power, my husband and I resigned our posts. We decided to leave Syria for Algeria, and arrived there at the beginning of the 1970s as political refugees. I came to understand what it meant to be a political refugee and live in exile, here in Algiers within a community of politicians exiled from their countries. But I could not bear the restricted life which had been marked out for me. I refused to obey the Party's orders, because they conflicted with my love of freedom. I refused to yield to my husband's authority. He was a carbon copy of my family and brothers. The relationship between us was one between master and slave. This unbalanced sexual relationship was to haunt me for a long time. My husband, like my family, made me feel that my body was shameful, that I must hide it, and that talking frankly about our relationship was sinful. My body could not stand this harassment. I soon fell ill and would have died from a botched operation had I not been taken to Paris.

In Paris I decided to throw myself into life with no weapon other than my will. I worked as a secretary, a nanny, and a saleswoman in a toy shop. I learned French. I began working by day and studying by night until I completed my doctorate in literature. It was during this unhappy time that I experienced the noble generosity of women, for only they stood by me. I discovered the cultural life of Paris. I discovered what it meant to be free in mind and body. My political views on events in Syria meant I was refused a passport and could not return home. Exile was the daily fate I lived with each dawn.

Men continued to frighten me. Each time I thought of having a relationship or found someone attractive, I withdrew in fear. I imagined the whole of Paris was full of men just waiting to kill me.

I started working as a journalist. Before leaving Syria, I had published a small anthology of poems entitled *Anashid li Imra'a la Ta'rif al-Farah* (Anthems for a Woman Who Does Not Know Happiness). That little book had made me a writer without my realising it. But journalism made me a daughter of my time. It sent me wherever there was an important story to cover. I had to observe everything, watch every move and not close my eyes for a second to what was happening to the human race. I tried to capture the present as it slid into history, to explain to my readers so that neither they nor I would forget.

Life in Paris brought my past into conflict with my present. It brought the East into conflict with the West, and the two waged a constant battle inside me. I longed for the East and I felt that everything and everyone I loved was on the other side of the Mediterranean.

There was a continual struggle between this yearning and the reality of my life. I became keenly aware of the differences between East and West and of the way they interlocked – two opposite poles both attracted to and repelled by each other in a massive confusion of love and hate, of sweetness and anguish. I refused to back out of this struggle or to take sides. It was as if I had first needed to destroy my identity in order that I might find it more clearly and thereafter cling to it more passionately.

I felt I was Arab to the point of madness; all my experience of prisons, forbidden writing, mystery, fate and loss had served to reinforce my identity. But I had decided deep down that I would continue to live in the West, for here I would have freedom and continue to wait for the time when an Arab city would accept me, the whole me, full of anger, madness and dreams of a free society. But I also knew that the West would not accept my cultural difference, everything I had brought from over there, from the distant Orient. So I struggled to find that Arab world which I called my homeland.

There I was, dazzled by the illustrious names of this century, of which I had become aware in Paris through searching for an answer to the basic question: "Who am I?" Was I Western with all the freedom it brought but living with laws, norms and values which were not necessarily my own? Or was I that girl who had escaped to freedom, who had fled from all chains? I decided that I would touch down in Paris, then let the planes carry me from one Arab city to another and let the cities clothe me. I would become a woman of Damascus, Baghdad, Beirut, Jerusalem, Haifa and Amman.

I became a citizen of all Arab cities, with all the love and anguish they contained, until these cities were strung out like beads on a rosary which I held with mystic passion while moving from a lecture on Roland Barthes to a meeting with Simone de Beauvoir and on to an argument on Marxism and democracy with Régis Debray. The torment and contradiction I felt between East and West took its most concrete form in my relationships with men.

When I started writing in French, I freed myself from the taboos of language, as my mother tongue is the language of all taboos. But I could not continue writing in that language so I went back to Arabic and produced two novels, *al-Watan fi-l-'Aynayn* (The Homeland) and *Man Yajruw' 'ala al-Shawq* (Who Dares to Yearn), as well as several other political and literary books.

I have always regarded writing as a painful subject because of my dual identity. But it is a suffering that brings pleasure and enjoyment. Whenever I sail across the text, I enter a world of pure meditation. There are no frontiers and I inhabit the text itself. I have often asked myself why I write when I am so far away from the Arab readers for whom I write. I pour a huge amount of energy into my writing. I frequently used to think that I wrote as part of my battle to change what I had lived through as a child. Then, little by little, I became aware of the simple truth: I write because I love writing and take pleasure in it. This does not mean that the enjoyment is not challenged by other forces, by argument and simply by other people. For me, every sentence is commitment, every newspaper article a historical commitment. Thus it becomes dangerous to enjoy writing on a continual basis because the pleasure is shot through with responsibility. In other words, it is no longer a completely free form of enjoyment. After *The Homeland* was published, I felt that what I was writing had an effect on Arab readers. I have frequently wished for a universal language, so that through writing I could convey my deepest thoughts to the people among whom I have lived in Paris and other European capitals. But I realise that such a language can only exist in a world of fantasy. Was it not Utopia, that great city, where entirely different languages coexisted without any conflict between them?

One question continues to haunt me still: where do I exist – in the East or in the West? I have tried hard not to distance myself from this question nor draw back from highlighting it.

And do I write feminist literature? This is a question which I have frequently been asked. During the conference on "Women and Creativity", several writers focused on the subject, which made me reconsider it. But after looking at my own experience, I came to the conclusion that I do not write feminist literature as it is generally understood among Arab women writers. My writing does not differ from that of men except in its details. Everyone has their own style. There are women who write like men and vice versa.

I think most of my readers are men, young men in particular. As a woman I enjoy reading Shakespeare and Dostoyevsky and can empathise with the emotions these men express because they spring from feelings common to all. I am afraid of the statement so frequently repeated by women: "Women are different from men." I fear it because it is impossible to talk about a feminist soul in music, painting, philosophy or science, or at least I cannot understand things in this way. I am quite sure that there is no difference between human beings. I read Marquez, bearing in mind everything that has been said about women, and I notice that everything I would like to write exists in Marquez's writings.

I am certain that women possess extraordinary strength, but ultimately it is a question of humanity. Chivalry, for example, is always described as a male attribute, while history shows the truth to be different. Women are no less chivalrous than men, as has been proved time and again in wars and resistance movements. So no, I do not believe there is such a thing as women's literature. What is more important is that women succeed in developing their capacities as human beings. I believe that attempting to imprison women inside their femininity creates obstacles which impede such development. Ways are needed to allow women to develop as human beings, rather than waste their time.

When I write, I do not know who I am because I write in spite of myself. It never occurs to me for one moment that I am presenting a feminist view of the world or that I am writing feminist literature. When Marie Curie observed physical phenomena through her microscope, she did not describe her observations as a woman's observations. Such a thought would never have occurred to her. I believe that, like science, literature draws on a particular level of the human mind, a level which ultimately bears no relation to the gender of the writer.

AROUSSIA NALOUTI

Born on Djerba Island, Tunisia in 1950, Aroussia Nalouti began her literary career in the 1970s. Publication of her work has extended beyond Tunisia into many Arab newspapers and magazines. Nalouti's major works include *Al Bu'd al-Khamis* (The Fifth Dimension), a collection of short stories published in 1975, two collections of children's books, *Juha* published in 1976, and *Bisbas* which followed in 1982, while her novel *Maratij* was published in 1985. Nalouti has also written two plays: *Al-Tawba* (The Repentance), which was an adaptation of *Abi al-'Ala' al-Ma'ari's Risalat al-Ghufran* (The Letter of Forgiveness), performed by the Sindbad Theatre Company in 1992, and *Tamashi*, performed by Tunisia's National Theatre Company in 1995. As a further example of the diversity of her talents, Nalouti wrote the script for Salma Bakr's 1985 film *Fi Bilad al-Taryyun* (In the Country of Taryyun). She is currently working on a new novel, *Tamas* (The Attic).

THE ESSENCE OF LANGUAGE

AROUSSIA NALOUTI

It is with the utmost difficulty that a woman writer talks about the act of writing, for this act is carried out in secret, far from the eyes of others. It is an utterly intimate and private act which distances you from those closest to you and something which you cannot allow to be seen until you are completely satisfied with it in one form or another. You see what the sculptor sees when he tries to create something perfect, or so you must believe if you try to bribe away the fatigue and repair the innermost cracks caused by excavating and penetrating the fragile core of self.

Writing is a wonderful, yet fearful activity – perhaps wonderful precisely because of the fear it contains. It is composed of moments where you stand alone before yourself, with neither support nor mediation. You stand naked with your honesty and fragility, weighed down by the burden of what is stored within and concealed. All that has happened and is happening there, within you, still remains. This terrible memory has lost nothing of former times; its files open themselves up to you from many different directions. Every pulse of the world is etched and tattooed on every bone in your body, as you crouch there like a terrified cat, confronted with the subterranean regions of your world.

In these terrible moments you may hold out against the flood, striving to find a place whose edges you may grasp; you may struggle to shape the words and say to them "be", but they escape. Then, after much hardship and drought, they may materialise, and it is then and then alone that you stumble into delirium, a delirium so overwhelming that momentarily you lose consciousness.

Why all this? For whom and for what? What is it that motivates me? In truth, I do not know. Usually, I do not ask myself these questions. It is an adventure into which I entered one day, whose deluge swept me away without ever anchoring me. Will I ever find land?

I presume, somewhat vaguely, that all I want is to seize some elusive sparkle, to grasp an extinct pulse and make it inhabit the paradise of words. It may be the enigma of existence that sends me to the grace of letters and words in search of meaning. It may be foolishness and ugliness which impel me to search for absent sources of beauty in the depths of the human soul. I do not know exactly, but I do know that I yearn and die with longing to embrace the hidden text, the text of all texts, the body of the pulsating language, the old, the new, the ancient, the modern, the silent, the raging, to discover all that is bestowed and is denied.

This utterly vulgar and fascinating language captivates me not simply in itself but with all the rhythms of time, forms of place, kaleidoscopes of human existence in daily life and major convulsions that it conveys and has conveyed. This language, which only lives in the pulse of a human being who is pledged to extinction, this language which will outlive him, is his making! It remains a sign that testifies to his presence and passing. It expands his life symbolically; just as he gave it birth, so it returns to give birth to him.

When I write, I fashion myself once more, fashion the world around me, build and destroy, deny and confirm, scatter what is gathered and gather what escapes me. Within me I carry others, with their incandescence and their ugliness, loving and hating them just as I both love and hate myself. All turbidity, this human clay – and no consolation! Or perhaps the sole consolation is contained in the ability to laugh at oneself, seeking the wonder of verification amidst the confusion, craving clarity in the midst of obscurity.

Perhaps all the wonder is contained here!

And perhaps this makes fashioning the text turn into an elusive or continually impossible act, for I stand in the pit of doubt and questioning, even sometimes in the hollow of desperation.

My despair is the despair of someone who constructs without a blueprint, constructs with language, within a language laden with a thousand turns and inclinations and which does not yield to you even when you have the illusion of having mastered it. It is here, obedient to your command. At the same time it possesses you and forces you to finish where you started but feel as if you were still running.

My affair with writing is a story of mystic passion. It has known moments of fulfilment when I possessed the impossible and looked into the bottomless chasm of knowledge, but it has also known much wailing and hunger, when I have stood in the wilderness that stretches towards nothingness and have exhausted the self.

All efforts are made within the complex and obscure body of language; the architecture of the narrative is made from and within it; characters are sculpted from the network of its symbols, events from its verbs, its tenses, its forms and declensions. It is what it is, the tenant of dictionaries and lexicons, prisoner of grammar and morphology, controlled neither by eloquence nor by its elaborations, for it is all this and not this. It contains a hollow that assaults your fears and pulse and existence, as if it did not exist before you or know anyone besides you and as if it is yours and yours alone. It is that wise woman stirring in the deepest heart of time and place, in the centre of being. The day I grasp some of her essence, I will be able to broach the subject of my innermost experience with writing.

NAWAL EL-SAADAWI

A graduate of the Faculty of Medicine at Cairo University, Nawal el-Saadawi has emerged as a leading international feminist, writer and activist with publications translated into over ten European languages as well as into Japanese, Indonesian, Persian and Turkish. El-Saadawi's experiences in practising general medicine and psychiatry in both rural and urban Egypt inspire much of her writing. Her candid discussions of the sexual exploitation and experiences of women, most notably in *Women and Sex*, 1969 led to her dismissal from the Ministry of Health and then to imprisonment under Sadat in 1981. This latter experience was to inspire her 1984 work *Memoirs from the Women's Prison*. El-Saadawi's determination to continue the struggle for women in her country has been met with much public and private hardship and oppression. The stress of living through two abusive marriages appears only to have strengthened her determination. The fact that el-Saadawi's name is today to be found on the death lists of a number of terrorist organisations has done nothing to stifle her voice. Having faced the government closure of two of her own magazines, *Health* and *Noon*, el-Saadawi is currently President of the Arab Women's Solidarity Association, an organisation which she founded in 1982, which has also been subjected to much government intervention. El-Saadawi's autobiography, *Auraqi Hayati* (My Life's Papers) 1995, is now available.

With over twenty-four books published along with a number of short stories, plays and personal memoirs, el-Saadawi has been awarded a string of literary honours, including the Literary Award by the Supreme Council for Arts and Social Sciences in 1974, the Literary Award of Gubran and the Arab Association of Australia Award both awarded in 1988. Her most recent works are *The Fall of the Imam* (1987), *Memoirs of a Child Called Soad* (1990), *Ganat and the Devil* (1991) and *Love in the Kingdom of Oil* (1993).

ALONE WITH PEN AND PAPER

NAWAL EL-SAADAWI

I write this statement from a small city in a country in Europe. It has been three months since I left Egypt, my house and my family. A journey far from homeland and roots. How much my homeland and roots have bestowed upon me. Ever since I picked up the pen over forty years ago, I have been living under an ominous threat within my homeland. The powers that be are not pleased with my writing. What is it that threatens them in what I write? Can the ruling system really be brought down by writing?

Three months have passed and I long for nothing from the past. My longing is directed towards the future. What shall I write in the coming months of exile? Shall I write my autobiography? Shall I write about that dark danger that threatens my life, that is sometimes expressed by the regime, sometimes by religion?

On 8 June 1992, a writer was assassinated in Egypt. Bullets were fired and the assailants escaped. At two o'clock the following morning, the government posted a special guard outside my house in order to protect me! From what? Nobody knows what is happening in our country, and the authorities conceal the truth from us. Why? Because knowledge is power and they want to deprive the people of that knowledge.

Between the authorities and myself there is an old enmity that dates back to the start of slavery, to the times when the Pharaohs ruled Egypt. Has the regime changed in Egypt since those ancient times? Why otherwise are the authorities afraid of the freedom of speech that rejects slavery? Is there a greater slavery than a person going to prison simply for freely writing his opinion? Is there a greater slavery than a person being threatened with death simply for taking up a pen and speaking his mind? And if the writer is a woman it is even worse?

In my childhood I was aware of the flaws in the system around me. I was punished for being more intelligent than my brother. My grandmother would raise her hands heavenward and call on God to turn me into a boy, for intelligence disfigures a girl's femininity. At the end of the school year when I passed with flying colours I would receive no congratulations from anyone. My mother would drag me into the kitchen to learn how to cook, for this was more important for my future than excellence in school.

Is it a flaw in the system or in the whole universe? For my mother said that it was God who favoured my brother over me even though my brother failed every year!

In my childhood, I picked up the pen and practised the letters and the words until I began to write. I used to wonder, if God was just, why was my brother preferred – I passed every year and he always failed.

The teacher of Arabic was not happy with my writing and always said to me, "Don't ever question things. You must only obey." The word "why" was forbidden, but since childhood I have not stopped repeating it. In childhood they told me that I would go to Hell for asking why, and today they tell me that I deserve to be threatened. "Why don't you live like other women?" This question has been fired at me all my life from everyone around me. But I saw that the lives of women were like those of slaves, ruled by only one law – obedience.

There is a curious hostility between myself and obedience. In my view, obedience is a vice, not a virtue. Obedience means lack of debate, lack of initiative, lack of self-expression.

Obedience is the height of vice because it robs a person of his mind, honour and humanity. What is a person without an opinion? I saw myself as a person whereas they saw me as a woman, a female. And it seems there is some difference between a person and a woman.

For forty years I walked a long and difficult path in order to prove to family and country that a woman and a person are one and the same; forty years trying to express myself, trying to conquer the inner fear of God, of father, husband, regime, minister, president. All these powers were united against me, against my feelings and my free thoughts.

When I was a child my illiterate peasant grandmother used to tell me that "with the mind God's justice is known". But the ruling authorities of the state behave as if God is not justice but rather tyranny – subjugation for the slave, the peasant, the woman and the poor.

The ruling authorities are secure because they own the publishing houses and institutions. They may manipulate the word of God according to their interests.

Every ruler in Egypt, from my childhood up until today, claims that God is on his side and protects him at every step. In my childhood, King Farouq called himself the pious king, and the sheikhs in the mosques asked God to lengthen his life. These sheikhs even managed to trace the lineage of this king to the Prophet Mohammed, thus King Farouq (the descendant of Mohammed Ali, the Albanian) became a descendant of the Prophet in the Arab peninsula.

After the banishment of King Farouq in 1952, things changed overnight: the pious king became the corrupt, decadent king – consort of women, ally of the Devil, lover of wine and slave to gambling.

When Gamal Abdel Nasser came to power, he became the just ruler sent by God to the Egyptian people to save them from slavery, imperialism, feudalism and greedy capitalism. But when Nasser died in 1970, he became the dictatorial autocrat who had brought defeat and shame on the Egyptian people.

When Sadat came to the throne, he was the faithful president who knew God and built a state of knowledge, faith and prosperity. After Sadat was assassinated in October 1981, he became the corrupt president who, under the influence of wine or hashish, brought greater poverty and foreign debts to the Egyptian people, and who in the name of democracy imprisoned all opposition leaders.

And today, there is another president on the throne, Hosni Mubarak, and it is he who is the pure president and saviour who will lead the country to liberation, true democracy, justice and prosperity. Who knows what they will say about him when he goes the way of the others.

Writers in Egypt are split into two groups: those who flatter the rulers and authorities and receive fame, glory and money; and those who try to express themselves and are rewarded with hurt and marginalisation or prison, banishment and starvation.

Ever since taking up the pen I have belonged to the latter group; we are a minority but our existence cannot be denied, we cannot be ignored. Most of the time our writings are banned and our voices cannot be heard on the radio or read in print – for the media is owned by the government and it is only those they find acceptable who are allowed to air their views.

I do not mind that the government in Egypt is displeased with me, for this is proof that I am taking the correct path and expressing my opinion without fear of punishment from the authorities.

What more can they do to me? I have experienced all kinds of government punishment. First I was sacked from my work, then imprisoned; thereafter I have endured constant threats of worse to come.

Nonetheless, my ability to express my free opinion is more precious to me than all the money of Croesus or the king's throne, because when I am dead and buried in my grave, I will take with me neither money nor throne.

I still remember my father's words when I was a child. He also rebelled against the authorities and against his bosses at work. He used to tell us that nobody could take worldly goods to the grave.

"All that we leave behind are good deeds," my father used to say, and this expression has been engraved on my mind ever since.

I want no worldly possessions, but I do want to leave good deeds behind, the books I have written, the views and thoughts contained in them, which advocate justice, freedom and love.

For me, God is justice, freedom and love. I hear the voice of God within me, not from radio stations or the tops of minarets.

The ruling authorities in our country try to use God against the people, against women, against the poor. So the religious trends have grown in recent years. They are political movements which co-operate publicly or secretly with the authorities. They are trying hard to pull us back, to reduce the Muslim religion to a veil over a woman's face, to a ritual devoid of meaning, to mere texts in books.

In my youth, my first husband told me that obedience to one's husband was like obedience to God; I refused to obey and preferred divorce to marriage.

In my second marriage, after I had begun writing and publishing my work, my second husband came and said angrily, "You must choose – me or your writing!"

The pen was more important to me than my husband since by way of the pen I was able to express myself and realise my humanity. My husband was incompatible with my humanity; my husband wanted to impose obedience and household servitude on me, things which a slave might accept but not a free person.

I found that the institution of marriage and its laws were nothing but the remains of slavery; it must be changed into a humanitarian institution built on love, justice and freedom, not on obedience and servitude.

I succeeded in establishing a new family after meeting my third husband, a family based on mutual support and equality, irrespective of sex or age.

In the atmosphere of this new family, I brought up my daughter Mona, who has become an outstanding writer with a style of her own, and my son 'Atif, a film director with a strong sense of his own individualism.

After three months away from my family, I feel I miss them, but it is a different longing. It does not motivate me to return, for I am now experiencing a new stage in my creative life, a stage of separation, of viewing my country from a distance, looking at it from all aspects. I am living through a phase of looking inside myself and contemplating my past life with greater depth. It is a stage of life in a foreign country where I am learning about the new.

With every journey abroad, I always used to return and tell myself that I could only write from my homeland, from inside the struggle, immersed in the battle for freedom, justice and love.

But now I am living a new phase. I now believe that I am able to write from any place either within or outside my homeland. Perhaps writing outside the homeland has more depth because it distances me somewhat from the conflicts and battles, and gives me more opportunity for deep contemplation and thought.

I do not know how long this phase will last. My life was, and still is, unsettled. I have not known stability in the traditional sense.

I believe that stability is incompatible with creativity, even though creativity requires some degree of stability. It is a tricky balance, but all creative balances are hard and contradictory.

Does anything more than danger stimulate our creativity? And does anything threaten our creativity more than danger?

Sometimes I feel that I have lived life to the full and that life has given me more than it has taken from me; sometimes quite the reverse.

I think about writing my life history. Perhaps it is feeling that one's life is threatened that makes one think about writing an auto-biography, for I have never thought about it before, being always preoccupied with other things.

But today, I face myself and my life for the first time, or perhaps for the second time, the first being in the autumn of 1981 inside a prison cell.

It is a new phase, like a new, large prison encompassing the whole world. I am living in the whole world but I am completely alone; all I have with me is pen and paper.

My life has always been so, alone with pen and paper.

FAWZIA RASHID

Fawzia Rashid has been writing fiction since 1977. However, her first major publication came in 1983 with her novel *al-Hisar* (The Siege) followed in 1990 by her novel *Tahawwulat al-Faris al-Gharib fi-l-Bilad al-'Ariyya* (The Metamorphoses of the Strange Knight in the Naked Country). In 1994 two of her collections of short stories, *Maraya al-Zil wa-l-Farah* (Mirrors of Shadow and Joy) and *Kayfa Sara al-Akhdaru Hajaran* (How the Green Turned into Stone) were published in one volume entitled *Ghaba fi-l-'Ara'* (A Forest in the Wilderness).

Rashid has worked as a journalist on the cultural pages of *Akhbar al-Khalij* newspaper in Sharja since 1984. She has also written a range of critical and literary articles for the Gulf and Arab press and has worked as a correspondent for a number of other newspapers in the region. Her short stories have been translated into English, German, Japanese and Danish. At present Rashid is living and working in Cairo.

WRITING AND THE PURSUIT
OF FEMALE IDENTITY

FAWZIA RASHID

Creativity is hard, rare and deeply absorbing. It is a singular and exceptional world which transports the talented person (man or woman) to a secret and mysterious universe which makes sense of the confusion of the world and of people's relationships to themselves and their surroundings. Thus the hallmark of the creative self is the showing of the dialectic and exploratory relationship with the internal and the external. This talent – as we all know – has its subjective and objective conditions, but the critics often ignore the objective conditions of the creative woman in order to diminish the subjective. Thus, the most serious difficulty for her is that her identity is manipulated by a demon who constantly seeks to undermine her and reaffirm her inferiority.

Furthermore, cultural and journalistic circles, which are mainly male, often repeat the accusation that the creativity of a woman is inferior to the creativity of a man because she is still a prisoner of her subjective world and has not yet managed to emerge into the space of objective thought and the great cosmos which the man deals with in his creativity. This statement is presented as the final and absolute judgement on the work of women and is repeated without any regard for the iniquitous conditions under which women have been obliged to live. It is as if the woman, whose shortcomings and inadequacies have been confirmed throughout the ages, is thus incapable of being suited to the rich world of creativity, a world which demands special faculties and boundless powers, vision and thoughts, particularly since creativity stands on the highest level of human endeavour and art. Even if the judgement is not final, it will still be tainted by deep reservation about the deficient and dissonant powers of woman. And perhaps this provocative judgement contains some element of truth. But the truth, in this case, is conditional on the development of woman's creativity at a particular stage, even though some insist on making it conclusive without taking circumstances into account. Thus, looking for the objective and "historical" nature of this judgement is important in order to take stock of what is ambiguous in it and because it has been a real and special concern in my experience of writing.

I was aware of this prejudice from the start and tried to go beyond this awareness without it becoming a paralysing complex. For hundreds of years the woman has been imprisoned in coercive prohibitions in all her personal, cultural, social and political manifestations to the extent that it was not acknowledged that she had a soul like a man! Even after the recognition of the woman's soul, this soul was considered to be in league with the Devil and prey to disgrace – witchcraft and evil – in other words the woman was a deformed, inhuman being. This perception has left a long legacy of legends, popular myths and social and personal heritage which distorted the image of the woman and her humanity. Even now when she demands full freedom she is considered a confused, frivolous and childish being, hostile to ancient institutions. These institutions will not recognise her demands, since the concept of her inadequacies and shortcomings is still prevalent, though in a different, more developed and sophisticated form.

This short summary is necessary, in my view, in order to understand the legitimacy of the confusion faced by the woman creator. All her human talents have been compressed into the narrow bottleneck of such beliefs, and for a long time the woman has been prevented from thinking about her humanity and true identity, let alone her creativity. It follows from this that now, only recently released – let us say recently because decades do not compare with the stretch of ages across time – her first creative noise when she puts her head out of this constricting bottle, is a scream, a scream which resembles the first scream of humanity at the beginning of its journey with expression when man wants to express his creative self. The first scream of humanity was ambiguous, disturbed, immature – the voice of a primitive. His expression of self, too, took the form of a mumble; the voice began with the first beat of music and song and has developed through time until it has now entered the realm of mature creativity associated with objectivity and universal human expression.

How then can woman, after her recent entry into the world of creativity, distance herself from expressing self-concerns smothered for hundreds of years, since her marginalisation still continues with ferocity and she remains a being treated as a mere body or womb? Despite this, the creative Arab woman has quickly tried to go beyond such expressions of self to the more spacious world of creative writing. This is a doubly difficult task as her recent entry into the presence and turmoil of life in its complete form has been compounded by the fact that woman has been kept essentially illiterate, reading and writing being considered to be outside her experiential needs. Her entry to creative experience was, and no doubt will be, marked by a sense of artistic shortcoming since it lacks the maturity that comes from practice in writing and practice through long combat with artistic expression itself. But this is its strength; it is without doubt a new experience and, naturally, the first scream must produce a scream of self which may be the self in absolute form. But it is also very rich because it exposes all the inherited ugliness, sediments and distortions which have been practised against her.

However, an important question appears to us for, really, we women writers want to go beyond what is merely possible, to achieve that which is preferable. Question: does the creative Arab woman still revolve in an orbit of limited and confined dimensions? And the answer: no, because women's writing today asserts the opposite of this and, in the coming years, will assert that she is more vigilant than previously thought in the search for creative, spiritual and intellectual maturity. Moreover her writing will not relinquish the treasure of her own personal experience. This vigilance of hers arises from the fact that she is trying hard to understand herself and her world and to consider the reason for the long legacy of marginalisation that still divests her of her right to full life and creativity. Her power of resistance will develop more and more, since the woman is intrinsically a creative being who possesses sensitivity and profound existential feelings which qualify her for true creativity, even while she remains tied by presumptions of inferiority and fettered by all the details of professional and household cares – the burden of motherhood and child-rearing, and the distortions of uneasy marital relations.

In my case, the search for mature creative existence was actually synonymous with the realisation of my full potential as a human being. Gulf countries and Bahrain, in particular, are splendid settings similar to the stories of *A Thousand and One Nights*, only without their beautiful wisdom and noble philosophy! Thus my human and creative emergence was subject to understanding the shortcomings surrounding the existence of women in the world in general, in the Arab and Muslim world in particular and more specifically in the Gulf. From then on the challenge presented itself in an infinite number of forms. There was the struggle between self-motivation and the forces that sought to suppress it – self-motivation achieved the desired result when it was greater than the powers of oppression. And there were times when creativity could only achieve the full power of its expression when it exploded from the self, a self pledged to truth and to decisive confrontation with the family and with social and political institutions. In this way expression could acquire its legitimacy and enter the realms of mature discussion and creativity.

Thus our feelings at the beginning were mixed – it seems that this is to be our fate as Arab women. The writing needed criticism, so concern for self was mixed with more general concerns, in particular that the personal should include political and human anxieties in the search for an identity that was truly universal. In writing it did not concern me that the realisation should be feminist in the limited subjective sense, but rather intellectual in the general sense, since in my view women's issues were always a part of local and international social issues and the conflict was not with men so much as with distorted and regressive inherited ideas which controlled both men and women.

Thus the notion of writing is the notion of searching for my own identity and the identity of men, both of which have been harmed. On the other hand, my involvement with journalism – cultural, intellectual and political writing – came to absorb the awareness which was expressed instantly.

The exploration of creative expression in the novel is different. This difference lies in the fact that the novel is an artistic form in itself with particular mechanisms and particular techniques, forms and styles which need to be mastered. The challenge was agitating, stimulating and tumultuous – I could either be a journalist and a novelist and apply meticulous attention to the difference between the two, or realise my potential within the restrictions that life imposes and be a journalist only, or finally adopt the conditions and mechanisms of creative writing and realise myself through literature.

This search for the perfect form and content of life and art and the difficult changes and transformations in Arab life happened in quick succession in the 1970s, the same time that I was opening my adolescent eyes to life.

When I wrote my first novel, *al-Hisar* (The Siege), in 1983, some critics considered it as the real beginning of fictional writing in Bahrain, as the novel *Zaynab* was in the Arab world. It was the first triumph I recorded in my humble creative notebook. The novel focuses on the social and political concerns which connect the love affair of a girl and a political prisoner with people and nation. In the same year, my collection of stories, *Maraya al-Zil wa-l-Farah* (Mirrors of Shadow and Joy), was published.

After this came the anthology, *Kayfa Sara al-Akhdaru Hajaran* (How the Green Turned into Stone). In this book I not only tried to express national concerns and issues, but also attempted to persevere in aspiring to artistic excellence. This is what later made me stop publishing my work for a number of years in order to develop a more defined form. The novel *Tahawwulat al-Faris al-Gharib fi-l-Bilad al-'Ariyya* (The Metamorphoses of the Strange Knight in the Naked Country) was written and rewritten four times in a period of five years and was well received by critics and writers because the contents were interwoven with a dense language; it also employed different techniques and interlocking time scales, in a novel which focused on Arab history since the fourth century *hijri* (Muslim calendar). For me, the contents were hard and new, but the challenge of technique was the hardest. It was a real departure from my early writing. Regretfully, some critics said that it was a novel that did not belong to women's writing – notice here the hidden persistence on the inferiority of women's writing even when she chooses subjects she is accused of not engaging with. They also said that had the name been deleted, they would have thought it to be the work of any male novelist, but it would not have occurred to them that the writer was a woman!

These words alone, despite their implications, are what strengthened my trust, not in myself but in women's writing in general, because I believe that other Arab women novelists have been told similar things about some of their novels.

I have said this not in order to brag but because I want to lift a heavy burden that has been lying on my chest, namely that the Arab woman has started to occupy a significant space on the writing map – the names there are now numerous. Women have joined me in exploring writing which is an expression of the concerns and issues of the contemporary creative woman and is not self-centred in a limited way – even though this is the image that is propagated.

Writing for a woman is the search for identity based on considering creativity as a real pursuit and not a luxury or intrusion on the world of "adults" who view her as an adolescent. The Arab woman writer, when she realises her rich potential, is nominated to enter the world of the novel through its widest doors. More than at any time in the past, she is now called upon to rectify the distorted image which has been replicated in many novels and films and television series, most of which are the product of male writers claiming that they are most capable of portraying women's internal world. Thus, her realisation of herself in the novel comes through the rich and sensitive contact with existence and invasion of the mysterious, unfathomable and fragile world of the imagination. Despite the mistaken assumption of her inferiority, despite accusations of personal immorality, despite fear, through her writing she nevertheless attempts the dismantling of taboo, and reveals the reality of the forbidden triad: sex, politics and religion.

The female line of descent has been considered a dangerous line. This frightening female had to be neutralised and enslaved, and the simplest way of ensuring this was to insist that she was inferior. Freudian psychoanalysis has played a dangerous role in affirming this, since the same actions which have taken place concerning female existence in the world since ancient times now take place today in relation to her creativity. The woman is called upon to understand her creative potential, rather than defend herself against the accusations being thrown at her. The woman is intuitive and capable of fathoming the secrets of creation because it takes its primary shape in her womb. Thus the woman is supposed to understand that her creativity is established because of her greater ability to identify and empathise with personal and social issues.

All critical writing that is exploring creativity in a serious way with regard to its relationship to the self rather than to gender is paving the way to new human understanding of creativity and of that female creativity which is fit to delve in greater depths into the universe. We are excellent at continually listening to our internal voices, for these voices have been newly liberated, and at exploring the unconscious freed from the distortions of history. This listening alone has the power to extract the most beautiful texts from us. The idea that women's writing is self-centred must be an expression of distinctiveness not of weakness or inadequacy, for this bridled self has the right to soar high in the first place and to expose the nature of the oppression practised against her. This should be associated with understanding the writing skills and various techniques which aid distinctive and excellent writing.

Every word uttered by a woman is important because it emerges from the jaws of long confinement in the prison of distorted thinking about the nature of women. The first noise to emerge from a prisoner is the sound of a long sigh expressing the pain accumulated whilst in prison. We must examine this first sigh seriously and faithfully since surely it will be followed by forms of real creativity. We realise the importance of the writing a woman creates, because she is in ascent on the wheel of time. The superiority of one sex over the other will be replaced with the humanisation of both sexes.

These words are not a war against man or against his creativity but rather an attempt to open arms out wide to the minds of men trying together with women to produce and form new ideas in which both rid themselves of a heritage which deformed not just both of them but also life itself. Both of them – man and woman – came to be at war with each other rather than uniting to create real peace between them, so that they could fight against erroneous ideas and against everything that contorts all that is beautiful between them. And this could only be done by ideas and literature. Concerning this pursuit of writing, I believe that the time has truly come for us as creative women to expel the vast store of pain and intellectual terror that has been practised against us as human beings and drive it towards a brighter terrain shining with creativity, not just as a mere token piercing this place for the first time but as a real entry into creative and fictional writing in general. We may only do this through more attention to the artistic forms which may shape our vast wealth of expertise and experience. In this regard, we are no longer simply concerned with what a woman says in her writing but also with how she says it and with how her creative self communicates itself to others. This means more deliberation and more observation of the linguistic and technical skills that distinguished literature has achieved.

We are indeed in need of putting all our artistic and intellectual concepts and theses into the intensive-care unit in order to nurture this awareness. It has been exhausted by a long distorted heritage, and so we must nurse it back to intellectual health and pursue the honest serious search for a world worthy of us and in which we are worthy, both creatively and humanely. I believe that this is the real challenge for women writers.

HADIA SAID

Hadia Said was born in Lebanon and has lived in Beirut, Baghdad and Rabat. She is currently living in London where she works as a journalist. Said's many articles and short stories have been published in a number of different Arab cultural journals. Her first collection of short stories, entitled *Ya Layl* (O Night), was published in 1978. *Urjuhat al-Mina'* (The Swing of the Port), her second collection, was published in 1981. By 1989 a further two volumes, *Rahil* (Departure) and *Nisa' Kharijat 'ala al-Nas* (Women Outside the Script), were to be added to her list of publications.

Said's writing has not been restricted to print. She has also written scripts for a number of documentary films for television and cinema. These include *Hikayt al-Sa'at al-Jamila* (The Tale of the Beautiful Hours), directed by Tariq Abd al-Karim in 1975 and awarded a prize by the Committee for the Defence of Peace in the Soviet Union, and *Tahqiq 'An Um-Hamid* (Investigating Um-Hamid) directed by 'Imad Bahjat, produced by the Institution for Cinema and Television in Baghdad in 1978 and also awarded a prize, this time by the Gulf Television Festival in Kuwait.

Hadia Said's novel *Bustan Aswad* (Black Orchard) was awarded the Katiba Magazine Literary Prize.

I KNEW HER WHEN SHE WROTE

HADIA SAID

⌁⌁⌁

I would like to tell you about her.

Can one differentiate a private life from a life of writing and creativity?

Her life was not so compartmentalised. She felt that the world was language and that language was a vast world. Cocooned within these feelings, she developed and learned the meaning of being alone in the company of her secret world.

Whatever the writing, whether thoughts, scribbles, bad poems or parts of the body of a still incomplete text, whatever its perspectives and objectives, all can stem from observations or cynical views, sometimes from encouragement or even from criticism. For her, however, it was something different. It was a storm-like love, a surge like a moment of passion.

She told me that in a time past, whilst playing in the gardens of her twenties, she had been unfaithful in different ways. For example, she could not conceal love's secret from the paper, and the pen would

often turn into another lover. In this way, without affectation or
artificiality, with the simplicity of a children's story, she said:

I love my love on paper.

When her first work was published, in the form of a story in a
literary magazine, one of her male relatives said to her: you have
disgraced the family. When she re-read her story she realised that she
had hidden memories in her mind which were recalled in moments of
distress. Everything that happened to her in writing was involuntary,
as if a genie inhabited her and dictated her expression.

But she was neither naïve nor stupid. As for knowledge, culture
and experience, she led a normal life. She said she was normal,
though some of those close to her claim that she was known for her
delicate feelings which at times bordered on the morbid, and that her
vivid imagination made her identify with terrible events. This was in
addition to her readings and her delight in everything that brought
knowledge and strength.

When a well-known publishing house published her first book,
a collection of stories, some people wrote that it was a novel with
different titles, others that it was a long short story in a number of
stages, or that it was stories about one personality. She was happy
and exuberant after the book was published. She cut out everything
written about it and carefully concealed the cuttings. Drunk with
happiness, she gave a little party in celebration and listened to the
flattery and praise. Writing was on the point of becoming a beautiful
journey glittering with celebrations, smiles and congratulations.

She did not know me very well then and I, in turn, did not feel
she was close enough for me to give her more attention, or care more
about her. For her, it was as if I had not yet been born, while for
me she was, well, I don't know, a child perhaps, or a cherished being.
Then, one evening she came to me in tears, after receiving her first
shock. At that moment, I felt that we were reaching a turning point.
She said that the man who was closest to her, some of whose features
had unwittingly escaped into her first book, had come to her, angry

and threatening. He had delivered a long speech from which she understood that she had reviled and betrayed him and that their secrets had been put under a spotlight.

When others read her book, she heard comments about courage and candour. But she was also met with gossip and slander. They said that among the daring expressions there was vulgarity. However, she was praised for paying attention to female sensibilities, to fighters and martyrs, and for the way her characters harmonised in their concerns, large and small.

This man was unconcerned with her book except for the glimpses it afforded of himself, while her relatives searched out the scandals so as to decide how much to censure her.

At this point, as the close friend and the other relatives discussed her writing, we stood together. Now the relationship took on another shape – a woman writes, someone close to her knows her and reads her because he knows her, and others, strangers, read her and she does not know how or why.

It was as if, before the book, she was at one with her ego. Language was a walled garden which could not be reached. What about circumstances, place and time?

It is all in the book: her, her city and her space, what she knows, what she is searching for and that labyrinth which possesses an astonishing and secret compass, sometimes known as talent or ability or singularity or even "another dimension".

It was as if that first book was a reaction, or the proceeds of agitations which expanded and had to explode. It was like temptation. She knew this temptation very well, and what it meant to her, from the time she had read St Paul's Epistle to his disciples. The saint's teaching, which concentrated on the arts of women, can be summarised thus: he wants them to clothe themselves in modesty and goodness, diffidence and gravity, not with plaited hair and gold, pearls and luxurious clothes but with the good works which are proper to women committed to obeying God. St Paul said that when women were learning, they should observe silence with total humility. He was resolute in his approval of the education of women but not of their ruling over men. Of course, he said that Adam was the one who was fashioned first, after which came Eve. Adam was not tempted, but rather it was the woman who was tempted and lapsed into disobedience.

It is true. St Paul was right. She followed his teachings fully, as she had received them, first from the Gospels taught by the nuns on the mountain where she had spent her childhood and youth, then while learning the True Religion (Islam), including the obligations, duties and the *Hadith*, the sayings of the Prophet. But writing tempted her and she fell into disobedience. St Paul himself recognises this inevitability. Her first book was like the first sin. She did not know it was a sin, only that she was enticed by the snake, the apple, compulsion and desire, yes desire, a love which could never be quenched, either secretly or openly. That first piece of writing was a first sin, with the innocence of the first touch and the first escape.

So we first encountered each other after this book had been written. It was no longer a matter of trying or of venting anger or of talent or a young woman writing or feeling happy. The matter became an issue, a responsibility, it became life. How did this happen?

I try to recall the moment we met, at the threshold of clarity, in front of age, history, gender, national concern, political torture, Beirut, Baghdad and Palestine. In short, awareness.

I believe that we met in a crowd, in the middle of a city clamouring with contradictions and tragedy. Circumstances brought us together with people who resembled us or whom we wished to resemble.

I did not have a ready prescription, nor did others. The transformation took place day by day, and we could only cling to what slipped out. All the happiness, the conflicts and wars between herself and the other, the man, the family, the world no longer mattered to the little girl who had now grown up. No longer was each secret or repression an opportunity for obduracy on paper or for writing a snare to avenge conflicts and injustices, small or innocent vices.

The pursuit of writing was a window with millions of shutters which opened every day, no, every moment, onto a new discovery. Memory was a vast storehouse feeding an awesome motor which ran on the power and energy that she felt when she came to take up writing as a career. She freed herself from the persistence of Qur'anic verses, instructions and sacred epistles. She began to know. She began to assess. She became a writer. She told me in a state of intoxication: I did not think it would be so easy. Where are the thorns they talk about? Where are the sacrifices, the bitterness, the disappointments and the snubs? Everyone is behind me. Some of them take my hand, some pat me on the shoulder and encourage me. Others write studies about me and introductions to my books.

Perhaps she did not finish the sentence, or perhaps she finished it while my mind was wandering. I did not tell her I was preoccupied. I did not open my heart and admit that I, for my part, had troubles, problems and concerns of my own, that this passion of hers for writing or for this seduction did not concern my every moment of the day, that I could not make myself part of her and forget myself, forget my life, my work, my worries over food and the whirlpool of love, marriage, childbirth and motherhood.

I too was busy and I abandoned her at a time, perhaps I regret it now, when I could have helped her. Why did what happened happen? Why did she present me her second book, crying and sobbing? Why did she yield to what was said to her after the first book and become afraid of what she was threatened with and embarrassed by her confessions? Why did she pile up her secrets in bundles of thick cloth, and content herself with untying the bundle little by little to let out no more than a secret or two? I failed. She said so while reading the introduction to her second book, a study written by a well-known critic. He called her to account over the time and place, he questioned her knowledge, urged her to be more profound and less hasty, and he pointed out incomplete stories, lack of clarity and characters which moved like shadows. She admitted that half the truth is insufficient and half a secret cannot live, and that the consideration and caution which had marked this book had let her down and stifled her – she had become covetous for things, not for her writing.

Like someone leaving a dark room for a garden of light, she went back to her book and rediscovered that she had not specified the time because the political situation had not allowed it. She had not specified the place as he had decreed, to ward off personal fears and embarrassment. And in drawing her characters, she had taken so-and-so's anger into consideration. All these things inflicted further punishment upon her. But this time, it was the punishment of fear and hesitation, a punishement for comitting the sin of creativity with neither tools nor weapons. Expression was no longer enough, with its warmth and sincerity; neither was suffering, whether drawn out or short. Now she must enter the area of the straight path. A rope may support an elephant or let a butterfly fall. The important thing was to maintain her equilibrium. It was like a pair of scales, which she had to learn to fine tune and balance.

Here another world opens up before her, another stage begins. Now she has reached a difficult region, a personal region – to be herself or not to be at all. She meets those who have preceded her and overtakes those who sparkled and were distinctive. She lives in the circle of the self and is shaken by the earthquake of all. She knows the connecting links between good people all the way to Palestine. She wears women's clothes like all women, but she has reached the region of art, the region of writing, the particular, the unique. And with the writer Tawfiq al-Hakim, she asks, "Yes, yes. What is art? What is art if not the artist himself?"

Here I had a much more intimate meeting with her. Here we agreed that she should become herself. She should write what she knew about and I would help her understand what writing was and the use of creativity. She was surrounded by men's opinions and observations, their admiration or displeasure. She read them and was sickened by their power. She benefited from their experience, learned from their schools and understood their methods. Every approach and contact was an opportunity to become more detached, to be in the midst of them, among them, behind them. It did not matter as long as she was herself, with her eyes, her views, her tongue, her pen, her fragrance and her femininity.

I had also passed through a stage. I had experienced development in my life, age and work. I had grown older and matured. I had known anguish great and small. So I said to her, okay, let us benefit together from what has happened. Let us devote ourselves to language, to sharp and concise phraseology, to expression without verbosity, to strength without affectation, to neutrality without blandness. Let us search for more knowledge from the mothers of books and the fathers of invention, from what we live on and what surrounds us. Let us learn how to bear the sorrows of the Arab nation the way we accept destiny and fate; let us learn from the separation from childhood and the separation from the lover, the peevishness of the husband and the peevishness of politics, the sweetness of love and the paradise of motherhood, all that has made us succumb to temptation and create novels.

So let it be. Thus we set out and so have matters progressed.

From her writing, to my life; from the truth of her secrets, to my fear, from her instinct, to my diffidence, and in another region, from my passion, to her unconscious, from my devotion, to the wounds of my city and the injury of my cause, to her emotions. So in all these things and others of which I know and of which she is ignorant, and from what she feels and which I record, the writer progresses and the woman withdraws. We have exchanged phases and roles. I was the pretty young girl whose history she had written. Then she became the pretty young girl and I gave birth to her and abandoned her.

From my life, she took my memories, and from hers, I took her practice and experience. She gave me the tenderness of love and I gave her the embrace of motherhood. I taught her and she taught me. In secret and surprisingly intimate moments, we laughed much when we remembered the saint's epistle. I would say "Since you were not allowed to teach me, how did you manage it?" She would say, "I wonder whether he enjoined that, before you bore your child and taught him?"

I now believe that we met each other in a more conscious and more intimate way while putting the final touches to the next novel. I claim that in this novel, provisionally called *Zaman al-Banat* (The Time of Girls), we have been able to reach an understanding on the following:

Writing took from my memory a very important and deep moment, the moment they call the discovery of love and the discovery of what I call the innocence of the first touch. Perhaps through her experience and her practice of writing, she discovered – in the novel, of course – that this moment which ends that paradise of primal innocence and starts to ignite and destroy what we used to call the unhappy consciousness, could also be applied to time and city and places and history. As for her as a writer, in this novel she started to work on what was beyond feeling and ego. On documentation. Documents from Beirut and the mountainous paradise it once was. As for myself as a woman, it was up to me to help her try to retrieve what was stored and piled up in my memory. I admit I found mountains and valleys of memories in rusty and locked boxes. At the moment of writing, when my memory was overgrown and dark, I would find the answer by turning to my daughter to see that she was continuing the journey and completing the circle. As a woman, I feel that my daughter completes me and that she has been able to recharge my memory on the one hand and provide a history of separate and continuous times on the other.

And yet, I do not know whether I have succeeded in my attempts to talk to you about the writer, about the person I knew when she wrote. Perhaps she was a part of me and perhaps I became part of her. Perhaps she will remain the writer and I will remain the woman, the female and the mother. As for the novel, it is what she lived and what I lived and what everyday life gives us to be recorded in writing.

ZHOR OUNISSI

Born in 1936 in the Algerian town of Constantine, Zhor Ounissi holds a BA in literature and philosophy. Ounissi's career has extended across a number of fields: teaching, journalism, and politics. She was a Member of the Algerian Parliament between 1977 and 1982 and became the first female minister in 1982 when she was appointed Minister for Social Affairs and National Guidance.

Her many publications include four collections of short stories: *Al-Rasif al-Na'im* (The Soft Pavement) published in 1967, *al-Zilal al-Mumtada* (Extending Shadows) published in 1982, *'Ala al-Shati' al-Akhar* (On the Other Shore) published in 1984 and *'Aja'iz al-Qamar* (Old Women of the Moon) published recently in Algeria. She has also published two novels, *Min Yaumiyyat Mudarrisa* (From the Diary of a Woman Teacher) in 1978 and *Lunja wa-l-Ghoul* (Lunja and the Ghoul) in 1995.

BIRTH OF A WRITER

ZHOR OUNISSI

ひののひ

How hard it is for the writer to introduce himself. An even harder exercise for a creative person to present a statement about himself – near impossible that it should be in the form of straightforward autobiography. The statement of a writer is bound to be creative since it does not emerge from a vacuum. Rather it comes after profound outpourings from the soul through the exercise of writing and the depiction of the human experience. I will try to present my experience as an author by depicting certain events, facts and people so that this experience loses neither its relationship to living reality nor its interaction with events, memory and history, nor the influence of a particular social, political and intellectual environment.

After this initial introduction, I will try to address some of the more important aspects of this experience – the experience of being a woman, the birth of a writer – in the form of tableaux, at times coloured, sometimes black and white, sometimes devoid of colour altogether. I offer you these tableaux in a spirit of exploration, information and mutual understanding.

Tableau One

Mankind is an intellect, a mind open to experience, with wide horizons whose foundations are constantly strengthened as he passes through new trials and experiences. Man is an idea and the idea itself is a review of things selected and valued from the past and the present with an eye to the future, so that in the end this intelligence will remain alive for ever, renewing itself, proceeding along the road of life.

Writing and creativity are a state of fantasy, tension and constant suffering. In all this, the most important role for the creative worker is to search unceasingly for the beautiful and joyful moments of human existence, for its most luminous and just aspects, its seasons of rejoicing and happiness, helping people to do away with the deformities and hollows which mar the beauty of life, to remove the seeds of despair by planting green shoots of hope where there is that despondency and loss which people have suffered down the ages. The creative person is a leader, one who has understood the secrets of life before others, so he must fly the human race to loftier worlds, taking off from reality, and in so doing exult in the eternal search for the most wonderful. The common man does not want the creative person to be a duplicate of himself, of his pains and hopes. He wants the creative writer to develop tools of expression and creativity. Hence the fantasy, tension and suffering implicit in the writer's task.

The process of writing and creativity has diverse and complex dimensions, especially when produced by a woman. Here, a particular suffering becomes clear, reflecting the need of the creative woman to broaden her inner world and keep up with the development of creativity.

Women everywhere in the world, not only in the Muslim Arab countries as everything is relative, live in a great dark prison, its foundations obsolete ideas, its walls sick, conservative minds, controlled by sadism and by every complex of those who came before us and those who come after us throughout the ages of intellectual decadence, the retreat of civilisation and human defeat.

Thus we find that, for a woman, writing is a life-long project, but it is a life which is aborted before it begins. The factors for its termination lie in its basic make-up. Factors for its obliteration combine with factors for its existence.

In the 1950s, when I began to be aware of myself, Algerian society was like many other Arab societies, a society suffering from colonialism, and the ignorance, poverty, sickness and fear this brought with it. The effects of the Second World War, with the sacrifice of thousands of our Algerian kinsfolk, and the joy of eventual victory, were of profound historical significance. The back of society was broken, the people had had the desire to rebel withdrawn from them; they had been deprived of their right to dream.

In this climate and at that time you could wander through that most beautiful of towns in east Algeria – Constantine – with its suspension bridges, and find that life was equally suspended. Girls younger than ten were considered women. They had no right to go out, to education, to joy or to childhood games; no, they had to start thinking about mastering cooking or weaving carpets and rugs, twisting their threads and strands. The only permitted dream was about a man, so that the realisation of the dream became an absolute goal, whatever his personality. He was a pillar, supporting a woman's life and representing all present and future aims for a woman.

Women were veiled in black. It is said that they wore black as they were in mourning for the daughters of the Virtuous, or that they dressed in black because of the victory of the Fatimids since this town and its outskirts were the target of their expansion. In both instances it appears that it was a stance in support of woman, but in reality it was a position imposed on her, a position of which she chose neither the colour nor the content.

In this climate and in this town where it was hard to find a sense of belonging, I started to explore the essence of writing. The threads binding the chrysalis unravelled, taking it from the dream to the abstract to the real – to free, expressive letters and to bold words that would lead to the publication in 1955 of my first story in the newspaper, *al-Basa'ir*, the mouthpiece of the Society of the Learned – all without any conscious effort on my part. The story had been the best essay in the national primary exams. I was 16 at the time. It was the result of attending a free school which taught Arabic language and ancient Islamic civilisation, subjects forbidden by the French administration. The schools, scattered here and there, were founded by Ibn Badis, a man of enormous intellect, standing and courage. He set in motion a peaceful and harmonious cultural renaissance supported by both men and women, providing knowledge and education for every member of society in the fight against ignorance. In his view, without this education there could be no renaissance, no freedom and no future. It was a movement which existed alongside other national movements. He took a chance on women over men and was once quoted as saying, "Whoever educates a man educates an individual. Whoever educates a woman educates a nation." But he died before his wager was realised, before winning the bet. Were those who came after him willing to continue to take chances? They added further conditions to the bet. We are for the progression of women, they said, and their education, but on condition that this is within a framework of religious and moral values. It is a civilised, clean and noble framework, but it still remains a framework and one which is always limited by its angles and dimensions. These conditions imposed on women were considered noble at the time, yet they were not imposed on men. Why? Is a woman more sacred than a man? Or was it because she is the vessel bearing the future man whose attributes they have already prescribed?

Tableau Two

When revolution broke out in my country, the basic threads of the Arabic language grew thicker; the weave showed its colour more clearly, awaiting the hand of a talented creator. And the desire to write grew stronger, stretching out across time and place. Of all the subjects the most pressing was the quest for freedom. In our country, freedom was something denied to both men and women, although the sexes differed in the extent to which they suffered from servitude. Men were enslaved but they vented their anger on their wives, daughters and sisters as they were the ones closest to them and over whom they were able to exert their authority. So women's enslavement was even greater, a slavery which was compounded several times over by the father, then the husband, then the son when he became a man.

In an essay entitled *Ta'widha min al-Janub* (Incantation from the South), I wrote:

> male children are the sons of women only while they are young, when they cry and wet themselves, and need care and attention. Once they have grown into young men and no longer need care or attention and can be boasted about to others, then they become the sons of men and men alone. When a man wishes to separate from his wife, he asks for custody of the boy but not the girl, even if she is of an age to understand and appreciate the meaning of paternity.

This practice ended with the outbreak of the revolution, the revolution to bring out creative energies, to bring feelings and sensations to light, to untie tongues, to liberate thoughts, to widen for me the circle of contemplation and the recording of thoughts and feelings which sometimes trickled, sometimes glided, were sometimes rebellious but often motionless when confronted with enormous obstacles causing them to stumble and hide but not stop.

In the history of any nation with an ancient civilisation there are huge historical moments which mark an age with a distinct character and leave the imprint of ideas on the minds of the following generations, and which are then transformed into an intellectual and historical phenomenon, which in length, breadth and depth surpasses the bounds of society and history. It would be wrong to judge any of these moments separately, ascribing too much or too little importance, for it is a mistake to set a value on just one part of the civilisation of this nation. I am referring here to the phenomenon of the heroism of Algerian women during the revolution of liberation. This is not the place for such exploration for it is a whole subject in itself and has been much researched and studied. But I will just say that the revolution, the woman and writing were like three springs each flowing into the other and drawing nourishment and existence from each other. These springs purified hearts and tongues and, for a time, smothered the narrow-mindedness of some men. Man saw a comrade for himself on the long road of revolution. He saw her in the mountain passes and the mists, cleaning out his septic wounds, providing him with pieces of bread and water, often the only rations available in those seven and a half cruel years, preferring to take the full force of the exploding bomb in order to protect him and his *mujahidin* comrades.

Woman is land and gift. Woman is freedom.

In a novel entitled *Min Yaumiyyat Mudarrisa* (From the Diary of a Woman Teacher), whose threads were rooted in the heart of independence, I wrote:

> Listen, woman. Genies ordered us to weave the rays of light into a plate of armour for your breast, to protect you and keep away the shivers of sudden cold, the phantom of death and loss. Angels have enjoined us to bear you on the wings of the wind to the Gardens of Paradise, for when you die, in reality you will not die, for your wound will be a wound for your enemies and the first lines on the peace document and another step on the road to freedom. At that time, the goddess of war will descend, and undo her braids as a symbol of defeat. Then she will throw herself at your feet, wash them with goodness and anoint them with oil. At that moment, you shall become freedom.

Tableau Three

When freedom came and the dawn of independence broke, repose from fighting imposed itself on everyone and highlighted other personal and public concerns. Algeria had changed. It had become free and this freedom which we so desired and sacrificed so much for has different needs. It does not need bombs to blow up a bridge or enemy barracks, but ploughs to till the soil, pickaxes to build and bridges to carry. Peace today does not only require strong forearms but also enlightened and ingenious minds in order to match the freedom of which we all dream. Algeria today needs the minds and arms of all its men and women. The university has opened its doors; many scholarships have been set aside for the men and women freedom fighters so they can acquire knowledge and complete the studies that stopped in 1956 under the slogan: "No education without freedom and no certificate without self-respect."

A period of education, learning and research is necessary for both women and men. The thrust of the revolution motivated resistance and persistence. The seats of learning became meeting places for the men and women freedom fighters, replacing the mountain precipices, city cellars and prison cells where they had all been previously kept. Algeria today needs everyone, just as it did in its recent past. In spite of this, discordant sounds are beginning to be heard over the horizon, sounds which echo once accepted ideas which had lain dormant. But these ideas have awoken and are being expressed in the cultural, political and social arena.

One day, a man sitting beside me on a university bench, said: "Are these ideas right? The woman played a most valuable role in the revolution but now she should rest. Let men serve her and return the favour. Enough wandering and loss. The comforts of home and marriage and raising children were denied her during the long years of revolution. She must make up for lost time." In spite of the good intentions of this man, it felt at the time as if the participation of woman in the service of her country, her sacrifices, martyrdom and dignity, had only been on loan to man and now he wished to return it because he wanted to fight on alone and, once again, have a monopoly on patriotism and the struggle for freedom.

Hence life consists of phases, and women had filled in some of the gaps in the phases but their natural place was in the home and nowhere else. This was the norm and anything else was abnormal.

But the dawn of independence was a light which overcame darkness; we must oppose such falsehoods. New battles await women, battles of a different kind which are perhaps more gruelling and have no guarantees of victory.

For me personally the most important field in these new battles was to move from grasping the basics of writing; this was a journey which would lead to maturity, to profusion and artistic creativity, to acquiring of experience in style and expression, and to courage in raising questions. I have believed from the outset that writing has an absolute unified strategy. In the process of creation, one must forget the duality of the sacred and the secular, the possible and the impossible, otherwise creativity becomes intimidating and its visible and invisible chains will strangle freedom of expression, the most important condition for writing.

Life overflows around me and the female secondary school students await the literature and philosophy class with enthusiasm and passion. They make me feel suddenly that I hold in my hands the reins of power, power over myself and even over those around me. Life overflows with giving, learning, knowledge and history; memory is the philosophy of life; revolution overcomes tyranny, fear and inertia. All these are living tributaries and subjects, strong with enthusiasm, which trigger inspiration, sharpen ideas and form a strong warm bond of friendship between me and my pen, a friendship which cannot be broken. It is a window opening onto hope, onto desire, onto construction, onto achievement.

I decided that it was necessary to sever my relations with any person unable to dream. Life is a dream and a programme. Some people do not have the capacity to dream, are unable to dream, even though dreaming is the first stage in the thinking process and thinking is human life. Such people, you find, prefer ready-made dreams and even if these dreams do not fit, it doesn't bother them. Those with no dreams have no life programme, nor even the outline of a programme related to life and renewal, to the hope of attaining a tomorrow to improve the present and future of mankind. Such people have no human values; they are the sons of ready-made fantasies. They are unable to understand the concerns of humanity, the concerns of culture, the concerns for change and renewal, the movement in search of the better and the loftier. The concerns of humanity do not stop them sleeping, do not torment them, though the torment starts in their homes, and the tormented are their mothers, wives and daughters.

It is a process of subjecting mankind to a supernatural authority by means of a terrestrial authority endowed with sanctity. And because the divine has a compassionate appearance in every heart, one could exploit it, in their opinion.

In the fourth chapter of my novel about my school-days I wrote:

> The girls left secondary school and I left at the same time to spend the rest of the day researching and questioning, driven by enthusiasm and determination. At the end of the day, I was content and put my tiny body to bed. There were no nightmares to disturb my sleep. I was intoxicated with wonderful optimistic feelings and in my sleep I saw a city made of transparent glass, rooted in the embrace of a golden dream, under a clear sky hung with stars. Cool air, fragrant with the scent of freedom, blew down its elegant streets; its places knew only smiles and felt only happiness. In the morning, I leapt out of bed, as though without a care in a world I had known for twenty years, radiant with its colour, bloom and clarity. I flew like a bird with wings of gold and boundless strength. I scattered smiles here and there, responsible for the well-being of everyone. I did not let myself be affected by the various scenes on my way to work every morning, neither the sickly old man hammering the heels of worn-out shoes, nor the emaciated young man behind the cart selling mint and chick peas, nor the barefoot young girl collecting cigarette butts, nor those pitiful slums which had borne enough of the earth's wretchedness to last throughout the present and the future.

Tableau Four

In 1970, I was invited to establish the first women's magazine in independent Algeria, as a forum for women's issues and concerns. This was an extremely important event at the time, affecting the living, social force of women throughout the country, women whose enthusiasm was being undermined by new and poisonous ideas that sought to diminish their militant role of the past.

Having worked in the national media since the dawn of independence, I did not much approve of the idea of specialisation and the practice of separating social issues into those concerning women and those concerning men, since social issues are one and the same. Nevertheless the social situation in our society and in other Arab societies overflowed with contradictions and intellectual and cultural debris that had a negative impact on the situation of women in particular, and this made me welcome the idea.

The magazine was to be a new platform in which we dealt with issues of women, the family and society in a literary and flexible style, without rhetorical flourishes or stipulations. It was a new platform which opened up wide horizons for me, acquainting me with the hidden aspects of society and its mentality, the most important of which was ignorance of Islam's teachings of tolerance. It showed me elements of progress and human development in a society which only knew the rituals of worship in Islam and its external signs. Colonialism crushed the concepts and fundamentals of this religion and its cultural values, such as the importance of freedom, learning and work.

Distortions and incitements created the wrong attitudes towards women and society. Investigations revealed the negative effects left by such issues as polygamy, arbitrary divorce, child custody, early marriage and women's work and a judiciary biased in favour of excessive or severe legislation; the whole process of distortions lasted twelve years.

At this time it so happened that such platforms proliferated and magazines diversified, so I decided to choose parliament as a more welcoming and significant platform. I was one of ten women elected to the law-making body in 1977: ten women among 260 men. Was it ten or one in twenty-six? I don't know. I only know that I found myself face to face with the legislative process in all fields of life – economic, social, intellectual and political.

I had two platforms, one achieved through writing, the other through legislation. I am a woman who has enjoyed the most productive periods through my working and intellectual life. Parliament is representation and I, together with the nine other doves, or eagles as we later became, did not just represent women or a particular party. Our representation took on a national character, which made the task more dangerous and difficult.

It so happened that a bill concerning family law came up before us which led to an intense struggle between the men and women deputies. The ten doves began by calling for peace, but then turned into sharp-clawed eagles. It is true that one of our popular proverbs says "One equals a thousand and a thousand is sufficient." But when a predominance of intellectual terrorism and verbal violence and sanctified opinion is given the authority, then logic and reason are lost together with the popular proverb.

The battle was long and heated. I shall only relate one incident to you. We had a colleague who from his appearance seemed to follow a Western, secular lifestyle, which was how we knew him. Suddenly, while we were discussing part of the Family Law Bill, we heard him calling on God to bear witness to his interventions and quoting verses from the Qur'an defending polygamy. We were astonished at the sudden change and began to examine the matter. Lo and behold, we found the man had several wives. Men do not mention religion unless they are addressing women's issues. This man wanted to draw up a law to suit his own requirements and meet his desires, ensuring that he could continue realising them. His cover for all this was a mistaken and biased interpretation of just, religious texts. Woman is a mere phantom which he conceals when he wants and parades when it suits him but is also one who keeps him awake when she rebels and torments him with recitations bearing the fragrance of freedom, a phantom that has to remain a follower, who cannot follow her own judgement or move of her own volition.

In the second chapter of *Lunja wa-l-Ghoul* (Lunja and the Ghoul), I wrote:

> Whoever has a daughter has a time bomb and to prevent the bomb exploding, you must hasten to place it in a safe place. To hide it and reduce it minimizes risk and preserves honour until that daughter may become a wife.

Thus have I seen some of them linking their sanctity to their wives. It is not to sanctify her but to maintain a monopoly of superiority and power through intellectual terrorism. Is that a man's complex?

In the first chapter of the novel I wrote:

They prevented him from crying and they prevented other men too. Why so? Isn't crying a feeling like any other? God created tears for both men and women, so why is a man forbidden them and why do we accuse him of lacking virility if he lets his tears fall? Weep Muhammad, weep, you are free, yes, free to do what you want. Are they not your tears? Are they not your eyes? It is not shameful for men to cry. Tears are a mercy and a relief for our anguish. Through tears you will reach the peak of manhood, the peak of humanity. You will take root in humanity. Then, after a short silence someone said: "The most important thing is that no one should see your tears!"

Tableau Five

The female doves unleashed a revolution when they discussed the clauses and contents of the Family Law Bill. They became hawks, eagles, tigresses. They exhausted themselves in order to achieve a bill that was both progressive and genuine, but it did not materialise. The obstacles were serious, even though the liberation revolution was considered to be one of the greatest revolutions of the modern world.

In the story *'Aja'iz al-Qamar* (Old Women of the Moon) I wrote:

A group of old women sit in front of the gates of the tomb of the holy man, Sidi Abd al-Rahman, chatting about this and that, each revealing her complaints to the other, as if they were the old women of the moon of popular legend. Their heads meet and their sighs and exuberances mingle so that good fortune and fate become the magical agent of all that happens to them. Hands make gestures with invisible meaning, or wipe a rebellious tear from the hardness of diseased eyelids so that it becomes a flood of tears shed for glory as yet unborn. Old people of the moon have thousands of stories which start with a woman and will only end with a woman who has not yet been placed in the womb of future time.

Following publication of this, I was invited to occupy a position as a member of the government, as the first woman minister in the history of Algeria.

Was this a punishment or a prize? Or was it a deliberate plan to keep me away from the field of battle, which almost deserved the popular proverb "One shall triumph over a thousand".

Such a position is a woman's right in our country, which she deserves and has achieved after a long and bitter battle and struggle. No man had anything to do with this achievement even if it may seem like that. It seems the regimes want to appear to be progressive and appreciative of a woman's struggles. It is a concession to women in general, but you are only a token.

These were the interpretations and advice given by my husband, relatives and friends when they noticed my hesitation and fear of this new mission.

And let me record here an important point. In this position, I tried with all intelligence and flexibility to impress on my ministerial colleagues and others in power that I was a mind in a female body. Yes, a female possessing a mind which had enabled her to succeed. My success has not been achieved through becoming a female man or a quasi-man. Describing a woman as being like a man is supposed proof of competence and human completeness, which is why I refused point-blank to disguise my femininity while doing this important job.

Was this good or bad? It was neither good nor bad, but a logical and necessary link in the complex chain of life.

To describe this important stage, lasting seven years, during which time I occupied two ministerial posts, and which was full of many lessons, decisions and experiences in the life of a creative woman requires time, wit and effort and will hopefully be achieved at some point in the future.

Tableau Six

I am now officially retired, retired from professional employment though not from writing. Today, I regard writing as the true work of the intellectual. I benefit from and review all that has happened in my private and professional life, the wealth and abundance of experience in different fields and throughout the most beautiful years of my life. All of it was a necessary and honest tributary of the creative stream, without which the creator cannot fashion a framework for himself. Every creative person must have a framework which is just and giving if it is to be directed towards the future within the movement of history, surpassing the present with an Eastern vision to participate in changing human life for the better. The time has gone when creative people and artists were regarded as aimless, introspective wanderers mulling over their dreams, isolated in their ivory towers, crying over their disappointments in life.

I would also like to address the subject of women's creativity. I personally feel neither ashamed nor inferior in any way when literature is classified as "women's literature" or "men's literature". However, this epithet should not be used as a way of assessing this literature – men's literature as good and women's literature as bad. I obtained degrees in philosophy and logic as well as literature, and wonder whether my literary experience made me closer to objectivity and reality rather than to daydreams, subjectivity and flying in worlds outside this country, or enfolded me in a small corner far from the important concerns of people, whether men or women.

It seems to me that time has gone beyond this story. It has become clear that the feminine form to which the sculptors of Arabic grammatical rules have paid so much attention is no longer a critical measure of the value of a creative writer. The presence of a letter denoting the feminine or masculine form does not necessarily define the gender of the artistic and intellectual work nor its literary merit and human worth. Good literature is not the monopoly of man, nor is bad literature the mere knitting and weaving of women.

The critical stage in which we live has eliminated many concepts and has changed priorities in discussion and struggle.

Some of you may be wondering why, then, I have quoted only passages reflecting women's issues even though these are not the only points I have addressed in my literary works. The answer is that this testimony has focused on the creative experience of women, taking into consideration the historical, social and intellectual circumstances in Arab society. I believe that every woman is creative, emanating from the richness of her experience as a fighter. The human creator must decide – should she stick to very private concerns or move away and reach beyond them to broader horizons, to the place where humanity exists?

And finally I would ask you: have I been able to touch upon the notion of searching for women's identity in my literary experience through this short sketch?

Perhaps yes, perhaps no. But the important thing is that despite the long road I still feel as if I am a feather carried by a strong gust of wind.

They placed the pen in the male sector of the chessboard, and the quill in the female, but they forgot that creativity began with a quill. And a quill, with its grace and lightness, will never break in the gusting winds.

CONCLUSION

❧☙

The following analysis is mainly thematic, providing a reading of the content of the "testimonies" anthologised. It will attempt to answer the following questions: How should the texts included in this anthology be classified? Are they, strictly speaking, some kind of self-representation or writing on writing? What is the truth value of these texts? How could a content analysis be carried out if the truth value cannot be established? Could we draw any conclusion about the psycho-social conditions of Arab women, their contribution to the national struggle and reformist movements within their respective societies? Could we classify Arab women writers who contributed to this anthology as "feminists"?

In autobiographical writing, which is essentially referential, writers negotiate "a narrative passage between the freedom of imaginative creation on the one hand and the constraints of biographical fact on the other."[1] This negotiation becomes even more delicate if the writer

---

1 Paul John Eakin, *Fiction in Autobiography* (Princeton, N.J., Princeton University Press, 1985), p. 3.

is an Arab woman writing within the Arab–Islamic culture. She tries to create an "I" out of diverse and possibly fictive material.

The intricate process of textual self-representation combines self-discovery, self-creation and self-perception and then representation within the constraints of the medium of language. This process turns the texts under discussion into narratives with a certain degree of fiction which varies according to the writing, writer's motives and the occasion.

Deciding where to draw the line between autobiography and fiction, and how the texts relate to the historical or political events they refer to, is a matter of speculation and assumes that the reader is familiar with these events, that he/she knows the "truth", or the "right" order of some of the events discussed. There are some parallels between the biographical information collected about each writer and their contribution to this volume, but more research needs to be done to establish overlaps or correspondence between the two.

All contributors to this book have created a "fictive" self, although some more than others. It is, therefore, impossible to establish the "truth" or "historical" value of these texts. "It is no longer necessary to decide whether this episode or that in autobiography is perfectly factual when the factual and the fictive alike are *intentional*."[2] The author of the autobiography has already selected some significant episodes from her past and the text is an interpretation of her personal experiences.

What adds to the challenge of pursuing truth in the testimonies is that they are not only, strictly speaking, segments of autobiographies, but are also writing on writing. The contributors are recounting a double history: that of self and that of becoming writers and practising writing. There are fragments of autobiographical information punc-tuated with the reasons behind choosing writing as a profession.

Most of the testimonies are an unfinished project or preludes to longer autobiographies. They are shorter than they should have been, and most of the story is left unsaid. Salwa Bakr's "Writing as a way

---

2 John Sturrock, *The Language of Autobiography* (Cambridge, Cambridge University Press, 1993), p. 287.

out" ends abruptly, leaving many issues untackled and many feelings unarticulated. The text touches upon Bakr's disillusionment with men and politics and why she has become a writer, but only in a superficial way.

Liana Badr begins her testimony by going back to her childhood when her mother discouraged her from looking at herself in the mirror, instilling that act with shame and guilt. The process of establishing the self as separate, and erecting boundaries between self and other is perceived as dangerous. That same process motivated her to become a writer. Her contribution to this volume is mainly a commentary on the composition of *The Eye of the Mirror*,[3] which is an epic novel based on the siege, followed by the massacre, of Tal el-Za'tar Palestinian refugee camp in Lebanon in 1975–6. In her testimony she shows that the research conducted on the history of Tal el-Za'tar goes hand in hand with the search for self and identity. The specific Palestinian "wound" and struggle for a homeland is combined with a much deeper existential pursuit.

Additionally, and as discussed in the introduction, many Arab women writers censor themselves. "The self that would reside at the centre of the text is decentred – and often is absent altogether – in women's autobiographical texts."[4] To be a woman autobiographer in most Arab societies is to try to repress or leave unsaid embarrassing or life-threatening arguments. The "Is" in the text are constructed carefully, with full awareness of being under the spotlight and of the role it has to play.

In "Writing away the prison" Hamida Na'na tries to put the record straight and justify why she has made certain choices in her life. She constructs a self that is both the narrator and main character. The self is shown in its social, political, religious and cultural inter-actions. This constructed self is basically a rebel which could not be confined by any institutions including that of marriage. It is a self carrying within it its own anguish and pursuit of liberty. It is a self that

---

3 Liana Badr, *The Eye of the Mirror* (Reading, Garnet Publishing, 1995).
4 Shari Benstock, *The Private Self: Theory and Practice of Women's Autobiographical Writings* (London, Routledge, 1988), p. 20.

wants more and seeks more and is unhappy with both living in Paris and going back to the Arab world. It is also a self faced with the dilemmas of belonging to a specific language and culture. Na'na constructs a self with the intention of inspiring the "young Arab men" who, she believes, constitute a large number of her audience: "I think most of my readers are men, young men in particular." Addressing this imaginary audience she writes, "For me, every sentence is a commitment, every newspaper article a historical commitment."[5]

Writing entails an intention, and the creative realisation of the intention, although it is likely to change in the course of the work. Although intention is a limitation, a specification of viewpoint, it is essential to get the process started and to guide overall shape. It is debatable whether the intention of the writer is ever realised. The intermediary is the process of realisation and the nature of the medium. Language, working in types and tokens, can only ever hint at specificity and can never be totally controlled. When writing, there is initially a synthetic, syncretic stage where words and images mix and fuse, and secondly there is an analytical editing stage. The logical mind paying attention to form and meaning clarifies the writing.

It is extremely difficult to establish the intentions of the women writers in this anthology. There are only two indicators to guide the reader: the reasons why the texts were written are clarified in the preface and the texts themselves. On a careful reading of both the Arabic original and the English the intentions of some of the writers become clear.

Barakat's writing in general, and her testimony in particular, show that G. W. Hegel's and Spinoza's concept of every determination as a negation had a profound impact on her. Her testimony is based on the equation that a more complete conception is one which embodies both the thing and its rival. Oppositional ideas coexist in any representation, whether of the self or in fiction. Her testimony moves away from self-representation towards commentary on writing and the motives

---

5 See this volume p. 102–3.

behind it. Writing is perhaps perceived – there are no certainties in Barakat's writings – as a desperate but paradoxical act of communication. The struggle is within the self in a narrative which is both self-effacement and glorification at the same time.

Turning the "I" in many paragraphs into "we", Barakat is trying to show that she is representative of other writers, whilst at the same time she only represents her individual self and narrates her own private point of view. Having no power and being non-partisan to political conflicts, the writer finds herself engrossed in this elusive act of writing, her only means of changing the social, cultural and philosophical system which she and others are products of.

Despite the above reading of Hoda Barakat's text it is still difficult to establish her intentions in writing it. The text was first read at the Multaqa al-Ibda' al-Nisa'i (Arab Women's Creativity Association) in Fes in 1992, so it was written with the awareness that the "self" constructed would be made public in front of a large Arab audience. Similarly, Alia Mamdouh presented her text at the Institut du Monde Arabe in Paris. Liana Badr, Zhor Ounissi, Fawzia Rashid and Samira al-Mana' also wrote their texts for public "consumption". So how did that affect their testimonies, if at all?

Despite the possible pitfalls of drawing comparisons between Arab women in the second half of the twentieth century and English women in the eighteenth and nineteenth centuries, I decided to take that risk. Although there are many cultural, social, religious and linguistic differences between the two, many of the conclusions drawn about eighteenth- and nineteenth-century English women apply to some of the writings of Arab women today. There might not be specific textual similarities between the writing of the two groups, except in the tension between domestic duties and writing. Inevitably this comparison is a reduction and simplification of both the history and writing of Victorian and eighteenth-century English women and that of contemporary Arab women. The following, therefore, should be seen within a certain context and should not be universalised.

Many full-length autobiographies and the texts of the testimonies by Arab women are cleansed of intimate encounters and socially unacceptable behaviour. "Repeatedly in writing by Victorian women, the intimate is marginalised, pushed to the very edge of their text, or restricted to incidental or fragmented expression in works purporting to be about something else."[6] Samira al-Mana' has not only marginalised the intimate but has also left it unarticulated; describing books, she writes, "books of romance and desire, of rose-tinted letters and love-nests, of the man whom all strive to keep her from touching."[7]

Similar to English women in the eighteenth and nineteenth centuries, contributors to this anthology and other women autobiographers generally feel that "their experiences were an unpardonable intrusion . . . using themselves more as case-histories than as unique examples of personality and achievement."[8] Their self-representation had to be justified by referring to political events, or by associating themselves with male members of the family who had played an important role in the public sphere. The above applies, to some extent, to the testimonies of Salwa Bakr, Hamida Na'na, Nawal el-Saadawi and Zhor Ounissi.

The self-fashioning of eighteenth-century women was "inevitably bound up in cultural definitions of gender as well as in their subversive thoughts and acts of resistance to those definitions."[9] All contributors to this anthology are aware of the roles defined for Arab women, and show how they rejected or resisted these roles. Ahlem Mosteghanemi, for example, says, "One morning I awoke to find myself a wife . . . cook, washerwoman, cleaner and nursemaid at all

6 Valerie Sanders, *The Private Lives of Victorian Women: Autobiography in Nineteenth-Century England* (London, Harvester Wheatsheaf, 1989), p. 15.
7 See this volume p. 76. "Rose" is the author's choice, but the original reads as *al-rasa'il al-zarqa'* (blue letters).
8 Valerie Sanders, *The Private Lives of Victorian Women: Autobiography in Nineteenth-Century England* (London, Harvester Wheatsheaf, 1989), p. 15.
9 Felicity A. Nussbaum, *The Autobiographical Subject: Gender and Ideology in Eighteenth-Century England* (London, The Johns Hopkins University Press, 1989), p. 133.

hours of the day. I had numerous roles and jobs, but I had lost the title of poet."[10]

The cultural definitions of gender begin early on when the woman writer is still a young girl. The testimonies reveal that Arab girls are moulded to be pleasant, obedient, silent and good housekeepers. Socially and culturally, a female is considered a potential dishonour for the family, and incomplete without *al-ka'in al-awhad* (the only recognised being), the man. Salwa Bakr writes, "I was brought up like millions of girls of my generation, with the idea that I had no existence without a man, the basic desire in the life of every girl. Thus she must be beautiful, gentle and elegant for the sake of a man."[11] Hamida Na'na writes, "When I was young, I realised that my primary concern had to be the man, which meant marriage and children . . . I realised I was a shameful being which ate and slept and lived."[12] To break out of the imposed mould, Arab women resort to what Samira al-Mana' calls "the splendid remedy which saved her grandmother Shahrazad from the claws of the villainous Shahrayar."[13]

Education comes after a struggle with the family and society. It is considered a luxury or even means to subversion in such hostile surroundings. "Girls younger than ten were considered women. They had no right to go out, to education, to joy or to childhood games,"[14] writes Zhor Ounissi. People tried to dissuade Na'na's mother from sending her to school, arguing that when she became literate, she would write love letters to men as a result, "I [Na'na] do know that my first day at school took on a funereal character at home. The family regarded it as sinful, and the neighbourhood ridiculed it."[15] Even Nawal el-Saadawi, who had a liberal upbringing, writes, "When I passed with flying colours I would receive no congratulations

10 See this volume pp. 84–5.
11 Ibid., p. 36.
12 Ibid., p. 94.
13 Ibid., p. 77.
14 Ibid., p. 145.
15 Ibid., p. 93.

from anyone. My mother would drag me into the kitchen to learn how to cook, for this was more important for my future than excellence in school."[16]

While being educated, while conforming to the acceptable definitions of gender, and while constructing a different role for themselves, the girls begin to grow up and show signs of becoming adolescent. A kind of panic ensues and a conflict between the daughter and the father, who perceives and imagines his daughter as activist, and inherently dangerous, and attempts to confine her. "In Islam there is no such belief in female inferiority. On the contrary, the whole system is based on the assumption that women are powerful and dangerous beings."[17] Women are perceived as *fitna*: disorder or chaos and their confinement becomes necessary not only to protect the women but also to protect the men.

These frantic attempts to police the women begin at the subconscious level. Fatina Sabah writes extensively about this subject in her book *Women in the Muslim Unconscious*. She argues that the oral and written traditions, including folk tales and the Qur'an, affect Muslim men's psyche and imagination. They learn to perceive women as activist and dangerous and as having to be confined and subjugated. The conflict between most women writers and their fathers or brothers, therefore, begins and probably continues for a lifetime.

"The father, the prototypical neopatriarchal figure, is the central agent of repression. His power and influence are 'grounded in punishment'."[18] Alia Mamdouh describes this neopatriarchal figure in most of her writing. "He [my father] was the first policeman – his profession – I had to face."[19] Na'na, after her older brother found a love letter addressed to her, was held prisoner in a dark room for

16 Ibid., p. 114.
17 Fatima Mernissi, *Beyond the Veil: Male–Female Dynamics in Modern Muslim Society* (London, Al-Saqi Books, 1985), p. 19.
18 Hisham Sharabi, *Neopatriarchy: a Theory of Distorted Change in Arab Society* (Oxford, Oxford University Press, 1988), p. 41.
19 See this volume p. 65.

more than fifteen days and was given a diet of dry bread or whatever her sister could "smuggle" to her.[20] Years later, in Colombia, when she stood, with her French husband, in the middle of the Alianos plain, she cried. Her husband could not understand. She felt that even that plain could not alleviate the feeling of captivity she carried with her ever since she had been locked up in the dark room. She discovered that the only way to freedom is to write away the prison.

Similar to English women in the eighteenth century most Arab women today live in societies where there is a "dichotomy between public passivity and private energy."[21] Women suffer from a constant internal conflict which might have serious psychological consequences. Through their writing, they try to control fear, which most of them grow up with. Alia Mamdouh describes this sense of fear: "It [fear] resides in our walls and foundations, in our vaults and our domes, between our keys and our locks . . . It is in every drawer, no head is free of it and its stamp is on every literary text."[22]

These social conditions lead women to develop a mainly silent public persona where they are pleasing, obedient girls, learning house-keeping, cooking and listening in silence to their fathers and brothers and then escaping whenever possible to an inner courtyard where they are the Shahrazad of their imaginary kingdom.

This disparity between the private and the public in women's lives opens up new spaces in the imagination. Na'na used to dream of a faraway land called Tunisia and the travelling of tribes and "that young man Sa'da had fallen in love with."[23] Alia Mamdouh rebelled against being cast as an invisible female and formed a free inner relationship with her spirit and mind: "During those years I became aware of the incongruity that existed between oppressive traditions

---

20 Ibid., p. 95.
21 Patricia Meyer Spacks, quoted by Felicity A. Nussbaum in *The Autobiographical Subject: Gender and Ideology in Eighteenth-Century England* (London, The Johns Hopkins University Press, 1989), p. 128.
22 See this volume p. 69
23 Ibid., p. 95.

and the bird who wanted to sing separately from the flock of boys and girls of the family . . . You have but one reservoir – your dreams."[24]

Many of the contributors to this anthology realise that the only way to survive a neopatriarchal society is to represent the neo-patriarch. They write them away in their novels and thus tame them. In *Mothballs*[25] the policeman father who causes fear in the hearts of his family attempts to commit suicide at the end. In *The Eye of the Mirror* Liana Badr creates a neopatriarch who is weak, defeated, broken, and relies on his wife and daughter for his survival. Hanan El-Sheikh, the Lebanese woman writer whose father refuses to read her novels, describes how the neopatriarch is defeated through writing, "My father, who used to threaten me with beating while pulling out his leather belt, was just a dove trembling in front of this novel and its black letters."[26]

The neopatriarch was not only the head of the family, he was also the head of the state and by representing him many women writers inevitably ended up in opposition, and participated in the fight not only against colonialism but also against despotic regimes. It is beyond the scope of this conclusion to present a history of women's political participation in the Arab world; however, their gradual disappointment with "grand" politics is evident in most of the texts included in this volume.

In their struggle to free themselves from Western colonialism many Arab countries gravitated towards the former Soviet Union. Socialist ideas spread among Arab intellectuals in the 1950s, 1960s and 1970s. Salwa Bakr became politicised as a child and took part in demonstrations against foreign rule as an adolescent. She classifies herself as a leftist revolutionary who fought against imperialism and oppression in the 1960s. In 1989 Bakr was imprisoned for alleged participation in the civil unrest at the Helwan Steel Works.

24 Ibid., p. 66.
25 Alia Mamdouh, *Mothballs* (Reading, Garnet Publishing, 1996).
26 Hanan El-Sheikh, "Fi Laylin Bahim", *Mawakif*, no. 69 (Autumn 1992), p. 53 (my translation).

After the collapse of the Soviet Union most Arab leftists went through a period of self-examination. In 1992, while Salwa Bakr was writing her contribution to this collection, Arab nationalism, propagated by Egypt's president, Gamal Abdel Nasser, was in regression after the Gulf War of 1990–1. Her testimony coincides with an historic moment of political self-examination and personal disillusionment. She argues that most political activists were opportunists who knew very little about the political ideologies they claimed to believe in and who used politics to gain money. She believes women resorted to conservatism as an admission of defeat and disillusionment with the political games men played around them.

Even earlier, Nawal el-Saadawi established herself as a Marxist-feminist and in most of her writing she draws parallels between classism and sexism. The woman in the traditional marriage institution is treated like a slave because of her gender. The slave must rebel against the master and the wife against her husband. In her book *al-Mar'ah wa-l-Jins*[27] she argued that women have equal rights to sexual pleasure; this caused a furore in most Arab countries, where her book was banned.

Nawal el-Saadawi lays the groundwork for an Arab feminist movement. She is a political and social activist, probably the nearest example to a suffragette in the Arab world. Although the Marxist-feminist discourse has been surpassed, el-Saadawi's importance is undisputed within the history of the women's liberation movement in the Arab world.

Unlike most of her writing, which is upbeat and defiant, her contribution to this book is reflective, with a tinge of sadness. It sheds light on her decision to leave Egypt when the campaign against writers and intellectuals reached unprecedented levels with the assassination of the Muslim liberal, Farag Fouda, in July 1992. Three months later el-Saadawi wrote this testimony in a "small city in a country in Europe". This autobiographical text has been followed by

---

27 Nawal el-Saadawi, *al-Mar'ah wa-l-Jins*, 3rd edn (Beirut, al-Mu'asasa al-'Arabiyya li-l-Dirasat, 1974).

a full-length autobiography, the autobiography which she was already contemplating when she wrote this piece.

The voice here is that of a lonely exiled writer who is taking stock of her past. The use of questions captures a moment of self-doubt. Although throughout her career el-Saadawi adhered rigidly to the teaching of Marxist-feminism she seems to be revising her views. She is repeating her beliefs to ward off serious self-examination. Loneliness reigns and living in exile brings to mind living in prison in 1981. She is face to face with herself as she begins to write her autobiography, *Awraqi Hayati*. Her contribution to this volume depicts clearly the moment her full-length autobiography was born.

"One of the unhappiest characteristics of this age is to have produced more refugees, migrants, displaced persons, and exiles than ever before in history."[28] Eight out of the thirteen contributors to this anthology live outside their countries of origin. The reasons for their forced or voluntary displacement vary and need to be researched further for satisfactory answers to be found.[29] Life in exile brings self-examination and uncertainty. The sense of identity is tested and readjusted while one lives away from the homeland. Exiles live in a state of continuous questioning and anguish that is almost irresolvable and irreversible.

Only recently Liana Badr, who was constantly on the move, was able to return to her homeland, Palestine, following the signature of the Declaration of Principles between the Palestine Liberation Organisation and Israel in 1993. After the end of the civil war in 1989 Hoda Barakat left Lebanon for France, where she now lives. Fadia Faqir has been living in self-imposed exile since 1986. Na'na has lived in Paris since the early 1980s. Although el-Saadawi was in self-imposed exile when she wrote her testimony, she has since returned to Egypt. Samira al-Mana' has been living in London since the early

---

28 Edward Said, *Culture and Imperialism* (London, Chatto and Windus, 1993), p. 402.
29 In *Culture and Imperialism* Edward Said differentiates between intellectuals who chose to live in exile and those who were forced to leave their countries (see pp. 402–7).

1970s. After the cancellation of the elections in Algeria in 1992, which was followed by civil unrest, Mosteghanemi could not go back to Algeria, and she now lives between Paris and Lebanon. The Bahraini writer Fawzia Rashid lives in Cairo. Hadia Said, the Lebanese writer, lives in London.

Fadia Faqir's testimony was written originally in English, then translated into Arabic to be presented at Fes. The audience this testimony is targeting is clearly Western and the author aims to present a counter-argument to the debates surrounding the Gulf war of 1990–1. The events discussed in this testimony were experienced by an Arab woman living in the West and are based on the portrayal of the Arab East in the Western media. Hence when compared to the other texts in this anthology, Faqir's writing is from the other side of the divide.

As an Arab writer, writing about Arab culture in English, Faqir is preoccupied with themes of exile and representation which reflect the condition of a writer who has crossed from one culture into another. The testimony shows how this trans-cultural position is reflected in the intricate process through which it was composed. Behind the all-embracing problems of creative duplicity, from a post-colonial position, emerges her struggle to comprehend an alien world and to cope with the challenge of surviving a bi-cultural identity.

In her anthologised testimony, and through Shahrazad who survived by telling tales, she describes her predicament of leaving her homeland, then ending up an émigré outside her group, living in self-imposed exile.

When she crossed from one language into another she did not anticipate a major conflict between the allied forces led by the US and Iraq. The Gulf war became the acid test for her sense of belonging to Britain, for it brought everything into question. It accelerated the speed of self-examination. Faqir lists the options open to her as a writer in exile: to write in English or to return to her native Arabic; to live in Britain or to return to Jordan, to belong to a group or to continue to live outside the safety and constraints of a group.

This testimony, although it shows that historical moment when the émigré comes face to face with herself and the choices she has made in her life, it fails to show the exile's resentment of non-exiles. The anguish and pain of separation from the original community are so great that the exile tends to overstate her/his predicament: "Wilfulness, exaggeration, overstatement: these are characteristic styles of being an exile, methods for compelling the world to accept your vision."[30] Paradoxically, Faqir's testimony is a cry to urge the host society to listen to those marginalised within it, but it is also an attempt to belong to the host society which comes across in her attempt to legitimise her ideas by quoting respectable writers and critics. "Shahrazad was screaming against this latest military adventure, but few people heard. Deafness, which was so eloquently described by John Berger, became endemic. She looked around her, tried to communicate, but got no response apart from polite smiles and small talk. Where does the bird fly after the last sky?"[31]

Ahlem Mosteghanemi's pain is neither exaggerated nor overstated. The beginnings of the civil war in Algeria between the Islamists and the government forces caused by the cancellation of the election of 1992, which were won by the Islamists, is the focus of Mosteghanemi's contribution to this anthology. Her testimony is a mixture of memories, anecdotes and commentary on writing leading to the present Algerian "distress".

Mosteghanemi begins her testimony by stating that to write is to cross the borders imposed by society. Writing means beginning to question, seeking to enlarge what it is possible to write and think, and for this reason the writer sets out on a perilous journey. Although she presents elements of self-history the testimony is preoccupied with a deeper pain over an Algeria described in her novel *Dhakirat al-Jasad* (The Body's Memory) as "pissing on its memory".[32]

Writing opens up forbidden rooms in the self. Having overcome the practical difficulties, Mosteghanemi was able to open up these

---

30 Edward Said, "Reflections on exile", *Granta 13* (Autumn 1984), pp. 167–8.
31 See this volume p. 58.
32 Ahlem Mosteghanemi, *Dhakirat al-Jasad* 2nd edn (Beirut, Dar al-Adab, 1996), p. 378 (my translation).

hidden spaces in the heart and write texts which push the limits of literature into the extreme. *Dhakirat al-Jasad* shows how she lives on the edge between the allowed and the prohibited, and how she keeps crossing the social, linguistic and religious borders.

That specific crossing of borders endangered not only Mosteghanemi's life, but those of other Algerian writers and journalists in the present climate of terror in Algeria. According to independent observers, 60,000 people were killed in the past five and a half years. The civil unrest has claimed the lives of sixty journalists and writers, many of them women.[33]

The regression in freedom of expression and what it is possible to write is lamented both in *Dhakirat al-Jasad* and in her contribution to this volume. With composed passion, Mosteghanemi describes the general state of defeat where dreams become so humble so quickly. To give a reading in Algeria and return home safe and sound becomes wishful thinking. To be an Algerian writer is to become a potential "martyr to Algerian writing"[34] and to learn to live with your death. To write becomes like shooting a bullet in the air, which might, with a twisted set of circumstances, change its course, pursue the writer and kill her: "Whereas we used to write dreaming of a country to die for, we now write for a country at whose hands we are dying . . . Twenty years ago I dreamed of one day receiving an invitation from Paris to deliver a lecture there. Today I hope to receive an invitation from Algeria to give that same lecture there and to return safely to my children."[35]

---

33 The statistics are taken from "Algeria fear and silence: a hidden human rights crisis", Amnesty International Report, MDE 28 November 1996. Although the report does not specify the number of women journalist killed so far, it cites the following two cases: Khadija Dahmani, a 28-year-old woman who wrote for the Arabic-language e*l-Chourouk el-Arabi* was shot dead on 5 December 1995; and Malika Sabur, a young woman journalist at the same newspaper was shot dead in front of her mother and family on 21 May 1995.

34 See this volume p. 89.

35 Ibid., p. 88.

Although Mosteghanemi's testimony shows the pain of living outside Algeria, she does not discuss the conflict in her country between government forces and different Islamic groups. She avoids engaging with the intricacies of a prolonged and senseless "civil war". Her position is equally unclear on the question of being a woman writer: "As for being a woman, that is my problem alone."[36] She resists tackling the question of Islamic revivalism head on and chooses to present it metaphorically by comparing it to a bullfight.

Na'na's position on the question of religion is similar to that of Nawal el-Saadawi and Zhor Ounissi. She argues that some neighbourhood sheikhs had a ready-made religious edict which stated that educating girls is forbidden. She looked into the Qur'an and the sayings of the Prophet (*Hadith*) to find their roots and couldn't. She believes that most of the restrictions against women are based on a misreading or an "ignorant" reading of religious texts. What men interpret as religious teachings, women see as a prescriptive and confining "misinterpretation" of the canons.

In her contribution to this volume, Hadia Said tackles the question of religion head on. At the beginning of her testimony she reveals the dual role she plays in her life: that of the woman and the writer. She shows how the writer and the woman living within a traditional society relate to each other and how the two establish contact through writing. Although a Muslim, Said uses Christian symbology and traditions to describe her position. The writer in her began writing because she was seduced by the Biblical apple, and she continued sinning on paper. Her first book came as a reaction to one of St Paul's epistles, in which he forbade women to teach and control men, and urged them to remain silent. He even went further by confirming that Eve was the one who was first seduced by the serpent and not Adam.

In her childhood and adolescence Said obeyed the teachings of St Paul until she committed the original sin of writing. At that moment she was reconciled with the writer in her and began a

---

36 Ibid., p. 84.

journey of struggle. When she became a professional writer she was able to free herself from all constraints, whether psychological, social or religious, ". . . while learning the True Religion (Islam), including the obligations, duties and the *Hadith*, the sayings of the Prophet. But writing tempted her and she fell into disobedience."[37]

Contributors to this anthology criticise Islamic practices from within the tradition and consider Islam as part of their culture. They made the choice of not rejecting the Islamic religion in its totality. They only reject misinterpretations of the Qur'an and the sayings of the Prophet (*Hadith*), and consider them either ignorant or exploitative. They fear being branded as Westernised which is associated with many social problems and with the experience of imperialism: "While 'modernization' is considered highly desirable, 'Westernization' is considered equally undesirable . . . They see 'emancipated' Muslim women as symbols of 'Westernization' which is linked [not only] with the colonization of Muslim peoples by Western powers in the not-too-distant past."[38]

There are parallels between the stigma attached to being "Westernised" and that attached to being a "feminist", which was translated relatively recently into Arabic as *al-nasawyya*. This might prove the Western origins of this concept, which has no roots in the Arab–Islamic culture and which has many colonial connotations. Like other Western concepts it was part and parcel of the colonial project: "When it came to the culture of other men, white supremacist views, androcentric and paternalistic convictions, and feminism came together in harmonious and actually entirely logical accord in the service of the imperial idea."[39]

As a result of challenging both the religious and political establishments women get penalised not only for being dissidents but also

---

37 Ibid., p. 136.
38 Riffat Hassan, "Feminist theology: the challenges for Muslim women," *Journal for Critical Studies of the Middle East*, no. 9 (Fall 1996), p. 57.
39 Leila Ahmed, *Women and Gender in Islam: Historical Roots of a Modern Debate* (London, Yale University Press, 1992), p. 152.

for being women. Despite their double jeopardy many Arab women writers refuse to classify themselves as "feminist". "They [several Arab women writers] complain of not wanting to be known as 'feminist' writers, but just as writers, not wanting to be renowned for their stance on women, but for their general outlook on life as well as the calibre of their prose."[40]

This refusal to associate themselves with "feminism" is due to many factors which need to be researched further. But if we have a quick look at some reviews, written by both female and male journalists or critics, of works written by women we can construct how women's writing is perceived in the Arab world today. Gender plays a major part in the reception of women writers' works where reviewers fail to subject it to objective, non-sexist and serious analysis and criticism. Salwa Bakr writes, "Male criticism does not pay attention to women's distinctive creativity . . . Women's creativity is seen, first and foremost, through male eyes."[41]

Two of the common characteristics of criticism of women's writing in the Arab world today are: (a) women's fiction has a gossipy quality about it and thus it is not art (b) women's writing is too personal in its content and has no value as literature. Male reviewers come to the texts written by women with preconceived ideas and assume a superior position to them. Most of the reviews of Hanan el-Sheikh's novels written by men are misogynist and patronising. A Lebanese male critic, al-Zughbi, describes el-Sheikh as "childlike" then goes on to write, "Having made her appearance in our literature, she [el-Sheikh] screams, she claws with long nails at everything hidden under our skin."[42]

Some male reviewers fail to distinguish between the women and their creative production, and see their work as an extension of

---

40 Elizabeth McKee, "The political agendas and textual strategies of Levantine women writers" in Mai Yamani, *Feminism and Islam: Legal and Literary Perspectives* (Reading, Ithaca Press, 1996), p. 134.
41 See this volume p. 38.
42 Edward Al-Zughbi, a review of *The Story of Zahra* in *an-Nahar* newspaper, Beirut, 11 April 1980.

themselves. They reduce the women writers to sex objects and fail to differentiate between their work and their bodies. The following is an extract from a review of Hanan el-Sheikh's novel, *The Story of Zahra*:[43] "A strange and unusual waterfall, liquid, humid, dark . . . may be that is why what we feel when we finish reading this book is exhaustion and a sensation of hot tears choking the throat . . . sticky nakedness . . . this book is pulsating . . . like volcanic eruptions . . . I have said very little about the book; but I want to say how much I admire Hanan el-Sheikh. Death is a lady of great charm whom Hanan cannot deal with except by flirting with her."[44]

Liana Badr, on the other hand, is accused of lack of creativity and of merely documenting what takes place around her in her novels. One of the reviewers of *The Eye of the Mirror* suggests that the novel would have been better structured without the anti-heroine, Aisha, who is in constant conflict with a male-dominated society. Criticising the presence of the author in the novel he writes, "the writer plays an important role in dividing the community," and then concludes by saying that the authorial voice "did not spoil the novel," thus contradicting himself.[45]

When the woman writer becomes unrepresentative of her sex, she is hailed as a good writer who has managed to transcend her gender. When reviewers approve of women's writing, they imply that she is really a man and that her writing belongs to a male, i.e. mainstream, literary tradition. In her novel *The Stone of Laughter*[46] Hoda Barakat has created a bisexual character at odds with the civil war in Lebanon. Her novel was praised by both male and female reviewers as genderless. A female reviewer, In'am Kachachi, wrote, "It is good news for a woman to write a *fahleh* [virile] novel, which

43 Hanan El-Sheikh, *The Story of Zahra* (London, Quartet Books, 1986).
44 Ounsi El-Haj, a review of *The Story of Zahra*, *an-Nahar* magazine, Paris, 5 May 1980.
45 'Umar Shabana, a review of *The Eye of the Mirror*, 13 March 1992.
46 Hoda Barakat, *The Stone of Laughter* (Reading, Garnet Publishing, 1995).

does not fall into the trap of 'feminist' literature. By breaking out, Barakat wrote a universal novel."[47] The implication in the word *fahleh* [virile], a term used to describe a sexually potent male, is that Barakat has become unrepresentative of her sex and has written a "masculine" novel.

Many women writers are afraid of being ghettoised in a culture which has preconceived ideas about what women's writing is about or should be. Yusif Idris, who was one of the best short-story writers and critics in Egypt, launched an attack on women writers like Hanan el-Sheikh and Alifa Rifaat, whose works were translated into English. The main idea behind Idris's attack is that women's writing gets published, translated and promoted because it is pornographic. "Some of the books by Arab women writers were chosen by Western publishing houses, only because they show the ugly sexual frustration which Muslim women suffer from . . . They are sexually explicit."[48]

It is no wonder, therefore, that many of the contributors to this anthology, like Ounissi, Barakat, Mamdouh and Na'na, reject or are ambivalent about being classified as either "feminist" or women writers, and about their writing being classified as women's literature. Na'na writes, "No, I do not believe there is such a thing as women's literature . . . I believe that attempting to imprison women inside their femininity creates obstacles which impede such development."[49]

The label "feminist" is associated with the colonial past, the hegemonic West, inferior literature, narrow-mindedness and political dogma in the Arab world. Miriam Cooke is aware of the pitfalls of using it and decides to coin a new term in her essay on Zaynab al-Ghazali, "I am using the term Islamic womanism[50] (*al-niswiya al-islamiya*) so as to avoid the race, class and north–south problems

---

47 In'am Kachachi, a review of *The Stone of Laughter*, *al-Dwaliyya* magazine, Paris, April 1991.
48 Yusif Idris, "al-Jins al-Islami", *al-Ahram* newspaper, 27 February 1989.
49 See this volume p. 103.
50 The term "womanism" was first used by Alice Walker in *In Search of Our Mother's Gardens: Womanist Prose* (London, The Women's Press, 1984), p. xi. She defines a womanist as a black feminist or feminist of colour who

inherent in the controversial term Islamic feminism (*al-unthawiyya al-islamiya*)."[51] The term *al-unthawiyya* has never been used in the Arab world to describe "feminism", in fact "feminism" is usually referred to as *nasawiyya* and womanism could be *mar'awiyya*.[52] But in order to get out of this impasse, indigenous concepts from within the culture, articulating women's subjectivity and their bid for autonomy, need to evolve in the native Arabic. Otherwise, any term coined outside the Arab world will always be viewed with suspicion and will fail to take root.

The task is even more complicated owing to the confusion in the use of language to describe the position of women in Arab societies. "A women's movement is required to call for an open and honest debate to examine the confusing and dangerous vocabulary used in discussing women, redefining and clarifying such words as 'modern', 'traditional', 'free', 'liberated' etc."[53] To open up forces for modernisation in Arab societies and encourage debate, not only do new terms need to be coined within the Arabic language, but also the old ones need to be re-examined and redefined.

Whether "feminists", "Muslim womanists", "advocators of equal rights" or not, the texts included in this anthology all show how hard it is for Arab women to practise writing. Like Mosteghanemi they become thieves, experts at stealing small hours to write. Their writing, their *raison d'être*, has to be presented as a marginal occupation within the powerful and predetermined social design. Like many Western

---

is "committed to survival and wholeness of all people, male and female. Not separatist."

51 Miriam Cooke, "Ayyam min Hayati: the prison memoirs of a Muslim sister", *Journal of Arabic Literature*, vol. xxvi, no. 1–2 (March–June 1995), p. 149.

52 The term *al-mar'awiyya* could be coined if grammatical rules of the Arabic language are broken, which might be considered unacceptable by some puritan grammarians.

53 Jean Said Makdisi, "The mythology of modernity: women and democracy in Lebanon", in Mai Yamani, *Feminism and Islam: Legal and Literary Perspectives* (Reading, Ithaca Press, 1996), p. 243.

women writers,[54] Arab women practise their profession in moments stolen away from their domestic duties. Many of them do not have a "room of their own", whether in the financial, geographical or temporal sense. Most of them write their alternative histories of the Arab world in isolation.

Arab women novelists who contributed to this volume should be seen within the context of a culture which discourages both men and women from exposing their private selves to the public, and as an acknowledgement of the desperate need on the part of some of them to write themselves and their lives in. For some it is a means of self-exploration, or self-affirmation or even self-promotion; for others these testimonies are an attempt to write histories of the homeland and their relationship with it. Some of the contributors find that their very identity is challenged by living in forced or self-imposed exile. Others are trying to exorcise the past in order to survive the present.

The texts of the testimonies anthologised are strikingly different and each author is presenting an individual experience in relation to the wider political and sociological arena in which she works. The voices here are distinct and unique. They all, however, perceive freedom as a prerequisite for writing, and show how that freedom is realised. For some it is the struggle with the family, the dominant neopatriarchy, for others it is the struggle with restrictive culture, oppressive regimes and/or the religious institution. Some fail to realise themselves in their countries of origin and choose to live in exile. And some end up displaced and uprooted, and for them any sense of personal or political freedom could not be achieved outside the homeland.

The thirteen Arab women included in this anthology, whose aspirations are different from those of the neopatriarchy, choose writing as a means of survival and resistance. They are women and they are writers and regardless of the discouragement they have faced they have created a vast and vital literary heritage. Writing for them is like

---

54 There are many Western women writers who find it difficult to practise writing, such as Tillie Olsen and Fay Weldon. See, for example, C. K. Stead (ed.), *The Letters and Journals of Katherine Mansfield: a selection* (Harmondsworth, Penguin, 1981).

being blessed with what Hélène Cixous describes as "a second heart". That second heart provides them with intellectual and linguistic nourishment, and helps them withstand the cycles of violence, the grand politics, the state of cultural stagnation, the tyranny in the family, the community and society at large, and even survive the restictions of the human condition.

Fadia Faqir
Durham
August 1997